The Flying Horses

TALES FROM CHINA

The Flying Horses

TALES FROM CHINA

Jo Manton
with verses in
the Chinese style
by Robert Gittings

Illustrated by Derek Collard

Holt, Rinehart and Winston
New York

First published in England by Methuen Children's Books Ltd.

Text copyright © 1977 by Jo Manton and Robert Gittings
Illustrations copyright © 1977 Methuen Children's Books Ltd.
Printed in the United States of America

10 9 8 7 6 5 4 3 2 1

Library of Congress Cataloging in Publication Data

Manton, Jo, 1919–
   The flying horses.
   SUMMARY: A retelling of Chinese folk tales that
span 4,000 years of that country's history.
   1. Tales, Chinese. [1. Folklore—China]
I. Gittings, Robert, joint author.   II. Collard,
Derek.   III. Title.
PZ8.1.M229Fl   823'.9'14   [398.2]   77-6344
ISBN 0-03-022701-1

Acknowledgement is made to Oxford University Press
who first published *The Peach Blossom Forest* in 1951,
from which several stories in this volume have been taken.

Contents

Introduction

These Chinese stories have been written for all who feel themselves drawn to distant times and places, yet hope to find when they arrive there not fantasy but a real world, with real men, women and children. The writers have made the journey delightedly, by many routes: through old pictures of buildings or landscape, people or fashions, through old stories told by word of mouth, histories written down centuries ago, or things large and small found by archaeologists today. The stories here are all taken from translations of real Chinese history and literature; the dialogue and poems often embody real Chinese sayings. They range in time from the earliest ancient popular legends which deal with the origins of the universe to a twentieth-century account of the Revolution.

The authors wish to thank the Suzallo Library, University of Washington, Seattle, USA, for that most Chinese of all pleasures – revisiting the past in books.

Jo Manton
Robert Gittings
Chichester 1977

1 · How the world was made

In the morning of time there was no sand, no sea, no cold blue waves, no tides to wash beneath the shining moon. There was no earth, no vast sky, no green or living thing – only a huge emptiness. Then an eggshell cracked and out stepped Pan Ku, who made the world.

He was a shaggy dwarf, with two horns on his head. Later he wore a bearskin in winter and a green leaf cloak in summer; but from the first he had a hammer and chisel and with these he set to work. He hammered and chiselled for eighteen-thousand years, making the heavens and the earth. Each day Pan Ku grew six feet taller than the day before, yet even so he needed help with his great task. So four fabulous beasts came to help him.

First a great flying lizard, the dragon, rose into the sky; there it beat its glittering scaly tail against the clouds and made rain.

Next came the phoenix bird with dazzling plumage. In olden days, they say, phoenixes would disport themselves on the terrace of a palace where music was being played, but nowadays, when there is nothing precious, phoenixes do not alight.

Next came the unicorn, with one horn in the centre of its forehead. It lives a thousand years, is loving to all men, and so gentle that a young girl can lead it with a silken thread.

Last came the tortoise, full of wisdom. To help Pan Ku, it held up the four corners of the earth on its four feet and solid shell.

These four and Pan Ku made the universe, but it was still empty.

Now came the time to clothe it with life. So Pan Ku dissolved, becoming the thing that he had made. His breath became the wind and clouds, his voice the thunder, his blood the rivers, his flesh the soil, his bones the rocks and precious stones. As for the fleas that lived in his shaggy hide, they hopped out and became our ancestors, the first men and women. Then the dragon made more rain, and wherever it fell on the hills and valleys of earth, ferny green grew in shoots curled like the phoenix tail; so for this reason dragon and phoenix are the friends of man. Colours were born; red in the morning sky, black in the cloud, green in the pine and white in the shining snow.

Yet the world still lived in darkness, for there was no day or night; the sun and the moon were still asleep at the bottom of the China Sea. So Pan Ku's ghost wrote the Chinese character for *sun* in his left hand and that for *moon* in his right. Then he went down to the white stony shore and, holding out each hand in turn, repeated a charm seven times. When they heard this, the sun and moon woke up and flew to their places in the sky. In the moon lives the moon queen, with a white hare which mixes the medicine of immortality in a white jade pestle and mortar. In the sun lives the sun king with his golden bird of dawning; every day at sunrise it gives a shrill cry. This celestial bird laid eggs which hatched cockerels with red wattles, who answer him every morning when he crows.

So with earth, sun, moon, men and women, day and night, the world was made; nor have any of these things changed since.

How lucky they were, those first people, who saw magical creatures, finned, footed and winged beyond the power of man to tell. They saw the surging dragons of the seas, the soaring of the phoenix in his flight, the leaping unicorn. Thunder was their drum, sun and moon their torches, stars their jewels. Blue air arched over them, or darkness drew its curtains; they wandered the freedom of the hills and smelt the scent of grass and water. The flame-coloured phoenix taught them fire, how to make pottery bowls and how to go on water in ships or on land in a cart with wheels. The tortoise, wrinkled philosopher, taught wisdom to anyone who would listen.

In time men and women grew clever; they learned to build, first houses, then cities in which to live. Yet still they loved the things Pan Ku and his fabulous beasts had made at the beginning of the world. They loved to hear tall pine-trees riding the night winds, or the bamboo's whisper on a summer evening. They loved to feel autumn rain fall in silk threads, to see white plum-blossom in spring, or the first snowfall of winter. So it happened once that a king stood by a pond watching wild geese on the water, when a great sage came riding by.

'Tell me, Great Sage,' said the king, 'do the wise and good also enjoy these things?'

'O King,' answered the sage, '*only* the wise and good know how to enjoy them.'

ANCIENT POPULAR LEGEND

Learn from this fable. Man,
The educated flea,
Can jump just so far as
His education allows.

2 · The river of stars

Look up into the sky at night. Silently through the dark jade vault flows a silver river of stars. Away on one side shines the Herdboy star and on the other the bright star of the Weaving Girl. There they hang in the sky, gazing across at each other, yet never able to touch or speak, for the river runs clear and cold between them. How did these stars take up their places in the sky? It is a tale the weaving-women tell; go ask any weaver as she sits at her loom.

Do the warp threads hang taut from the crossbar? Does the treadle answer my foot? Does the shuttle fly straight from my hand? Then my tale can begin.

'Once upon a time there was a herdboy who took service with a farmer to herd the beasts. He was poorer than the watchdog at the gate. At night he slept with the ox in its stall, smoke creeping through the thatch as he cooked his bean soup. In the morning he straddled the ox with naked feet and drove his herd out to graze on the hills. Through the holes in his coat the river wind blew, through his tattered straw hat the mountain rain poured. Yet far across the fields you could hear the tune he played on his bamboo flute. And not one of the rich farmers or cunning merchants for miles around could compare with this ragged cowboy on his great yellow ox.

'Off he went on the ox one morning to the hills, pushing through tangled thornbushes, up the mountain path. Then the golden ox spoke, in a human voice. "Today is the Seventh Day of the Seventh Moon. Now the Jade Emperor of the sky has nine beautiful daughters, and they come this day to swim in the lake. Honoured young master, since we share the same straw, I will tell you. Steal the clothes of one daughter and hide them, so you may become her husband and live in the sky for ever."

' "How shall I find her?" asked the herdboy amazed, for he had never heard an ox speak before.

' "Young sir, I will show you," said the golden ox.

'Then clouds began to stream from its hoofs and it soared into the air, flying through space with a whistling wind. They landed by a green lake, where nine lovely girls were bathing among water-lilies. The air was full of their laughter and their rainbow clothes lay in heaps on the shore.

' "See the red robes?" said the ox. "They belong to Seventh Daughter. She sits at her loom in the sky with threads fine-drawn and shuttle flying from hand to hand, and there she weaves the cloud silk of heaven. Grey satin of rain, white muslin of air, tender green clouds of evening – all are made on the Weaver Girl's loom. She sits and weaves from one year to the next, with only this one day holiday."

' "How slender her clever fingers!" whispered the herdboy. "How lovely her cloudy hair!"

' "Take her clothes and hide them under this willow-tree," said the ox. "Do not give them back until she promises to be your wife."

'So the herdboy seized the robe and sash and hid them in the willow's twisted roots. Eight daughters came out, drew on their scented robes and flew away, while the Weaving Girl still searched for hers.

' "Do not be afraid of this lowly person," said the herdboy, stepping out of hiding; but already the girl, blushing deeply, had dived to hide herself among the broad lily-leaves. "Promise me to become my wife," said the herdboy boldly, "and you shall have your clothes again."

'At first the Weaving Girl was frightened, but the ox and the willow-tree both spoke up to persuade her.

' "This marriage was made in heaven," said the ox, while the willow-tree whispered an old song:

Now the Seventh Day has come
The Herdboy leads the Weaver home.

'So in the end they were married in the Sky Palace, with bells and drums, with sweet cakes cooked on hot stones, and made ready to live happily ever after.

'Yet alas – this was not the end of their story.

'For the Weaving Girl had always been loving and dutiful to her father, the Emperor of the Sky, sitting hour after hour at her loom to weave his cloud silk. Yet now, from love of the herdboy, she gave up weaving and spent her days and nights in play and idle talk with him; no village girl could have been sillier in love than this daughter of the sky. So the silk clouds lay heaped up in airy disorder, shreds and tatters of grey and gold, blue sky at midnight and darkness at noon, rain at harvest and sunshine on the yellow leaves of autumn.

'Then the Jade Emperor grew angry. "It is this husband who has turned her head!" he said. "The couple must part. Then she will come to her senses, and do the work which fate has set her, not only to weave my cloud silk but to teach the crafts of spinning and weaving to all the women of China." So he turned the two lovers out of the Sky Palace, and plucking one of the silver pins from the girl's hair drew a line with it right across the dark vault of the night. Swiftly, silently the silver river of stars began to flow between them.

' "Husband, husband!" cried the Weaver Girl. She held out her arms to him, while her bitter tears fell down the sky like streaming rain. The herdboy tried bravely to swim across to her, but fate held him fixed in his own star.

'At the sight of his daughter's tears the Jade Emperor of the Sky relented. "You may meet once every year on the Seventh Night of the Seventh Month," he ordered.

' "But how shall I reach my herdboy?" cried the Weaving Girl.

' "I order all the magpies in the world of men to fly together and make a bridge, wing to wing, across the River of Stars. On that night only you may go safely across," said the Emperor.

'And so it happens. On summer evenings comes the squeak of

bats which flicker to and fro outside the house; the moonlight steals through the courtyard and in at the window. You could pluck stars by the handful, so clear is the sky. Then, on the Seventh Night, the magpies come in joyful flocks; wheeling and circling in the sky they take up their places in the bird-bridge. Hush! for she comes, tiny feet on soft plumage, heart fluttering louder than the birds' wings, safe into the arms of her lover. For one night and day they are together again.

'Next evening it often rains, a clear, fine, summer rain, like threads of silk from soft clouds. Then we women working at our looms, stamping our foot on the treadle, keeping straight the threads of warp and weft, look up into the sky. And we say to one another, as we throw the clacking shuttle: "Those are the tears which the Herdboy and the Weaving Girl shed at their parting across the River of Stars." '

ANCIENT POPULAR LEGEND

Each stone a star, whitely the river runs;
Nightly the parted lovers seek the brink,
Sigh, dare not. Even one whole day
Cannot atone ten thousand wasted hours.

3 · Lady into silkworm

Long ago in the Kingdom of Shu, where the Yellow River rises, lived a landowner with his wife and only child. This girl, Tsan Nu, was fourteen years old, too young to wear the black slippers of a lady; her bare feet in sandals were white as frost and her two glossy plaits not yet braided into one. Her gauze sleeves fluttered in the wind when she ran.

All the pleasures of country life were Tsan Nu's to enjoy. She sailed a boat on the lake, flew her dragon-kite in autumn gales, or drove her father's strong, deep-chested black horse in a red cart. Even this fiery creature trod softly when it felt Tsan Nu's light hand on the reins. At other times she lay in the garden under an old tree, watching the clouds sail by, or fished with her father by moonlight where the clear stream runs cold. On fine evenings she took her tame singing-bird out for a walk and a feast of sunflower seeds; in winter she gave picnics for her friends to enjoy the snow. Rainy hours filled themselves with lute or book. The whole family had no need to toil for treasure; within themselves they had the pearl of happiness.

Sudden as a thunder-clap at end of harvest, all this happiness vanished. For Tsan Nu's father, travelling in his carrying-chair to pay his land tax, was kidnapped by a band of robbers. For a whole year there was no word of him. His horse in the stable tossed its mane and fretted as though impatient for its master to return. His wife offered a rich reward for news, or a letter carved on a sliver of bamboo to say that he still lived. As for Tsan Nu, she was desolate. Day after day she climbed the hill to watch for a letter, in vain. The sight of his fan, his ink-slab, his writing-brush, brought quick tears to her eyes. At night she could not sleep, but stood at the window watching the moonlight creep through the great gate across the court. Her eyes were red with tears. She tore the gold pins from her hair and threw them on the floor, sobbing.

Nor would she eat. Useless to tempt her with melon soup or wild birds' eggs; she refused them all, till the sash round her waist slipped down to her hips. By her fifteenth birthday Tsan Nu was thin and pale as a petal.

Then her mother, in despair, said, 'My daughter is fifteen years old, of age to be married. I promise by Air, Fire and Water to give her in marriage to the one who can bring her father home.'

No young man in embroidered coat came to take up the challenge. But the black horse in the stable heard these words and stamped impatiently, tugging at its halter. The grooms closed the stable door, but by next morning the door was kicked down, the halter broken and the horse gone, no one knew where.

Three mornings later it came back in the first light when the moon was waning and distant temple bells sounded through the frosty air. Proudly the horse trotted through the rustling yellow leaves and in at the great gate of the house. There on its back, bruised, scratched, wild-haired and in fluttering rags, but alive, was Tsan Nu's father. Then there was happiness in the house again with feasting and dancing and music of bells and drums. The father told how he had escaped from the robbers but wandered in the forest, lost and starving, until the faithful horse galloped to his rescue. 'Now we can all be happy again and drink the good red wine,' he said.

Yet this was not to be. For in the stable the black horse neighed incessantly. The grooms tempted it with beans and barley, but it would not eat. And whenever Tsan Nu crossed the courtyard, the horse plunged and reared, stamping the stones till the sparks flew up. At last Tsan Nu's mother grew frightened, and at night, within the bed-curtains, she confessed the promise she had given.

'How was this foolish, unhappy person to know the horse would listen?' she cried in despair. 'Must we give him Tsan Nu as wife?'

'An oath made to men is not made to horses,' replied the landowner stoutly. 'And besides, a young girl cannot marry a horse. Say nothing to our daughter and the beast will forget its folly.'

The horse refused to forget and struggled more wildly than ever, rearing and stamping as though stung by a gadfly. When the grooms saddled him to ride, the horse would not answer to bridle or bit, but followed, breathing softly, wherever it heard the swish of Tsan Nu's skirts. Lowering its proud head, it licked the young girl's feet, as though it wanted to speak. At last the owner lost his temper.

'Will no one silence that brute?' he shouted. Then, snatching up his black bow, he shot the faithful horse through the heart. He took his sharp hunting knife, flayed the corpse, and spread the hide in the sun outside the gateway to dry. 'Now we shall have peace in our courtyard,' he said, and went back to the bamboo tallies of green tea-bushes and grain in his farm office. He had forgotten the saying that he who rides a tiger cannot dismount.

For next day Tsan Nu passed by. She was going to the apricot orchard with the farm maids, carrying flat baskets to fill with fruit, sleeves brushing the green boughs. As she passed by, the glossy black hide twitched, stirred, came to life, rose up and wrapped itself round her. Before she could struggle or cry the horse leaped into the air and soared to the clouds, carrying Tsan Nu wrapped within its own skin. The maids ran to tell her parents and then what weeping, as never before!

'Oh soul, come back!' they cried from the housetop. 'Why have you left your dwelling? Go not to the Land of Darkness! Oh soul, come back to your home! You shall have braids and ribbons, maids to serve you, feather beds, curtains of scarlet, rings of gold and jade! Tsan Nu, come back to your home!' But the blue air was empty and no girl's voice replied.

They searched everywhere and after ten days they found the hide. Deep in the orchard grew a mulberry tree, grey and twisted, gnarled fists of branches, thick-set leaves. At the foot of this tree lay the empty crumpled hide. And there, on a leaf, pointed little mouth swaying from side to side in a ceaseless search for food, lay a grey silkworm with the face of Tsan Nu. They could even hear the tiny rustle and crunch of her jaws as she chewed. Even as they watched, she began to vanish, steadily spinning herself a filament of pure white, wild silk to make a cocoon. When the cocoon had closed over her face, the parents brushed it gently off with a goose-feather and sorrowfully took home all that seemed left of their daughter.

Yet Tsan Nu came to them again at sunset, as they sat sorrowfully on their western terrace in the last red gleam. She came out of the tender clouds, dressed in rainbow silks and riding on her faithful lover, the horse. Slippers of red silk were on her feet, her moth brows painted black, jade in her hair. Round her flew phoenix birds and fairy servants, thick as snowflakes.

'Honoured parents, do not grieve for your unworthy daughter Tsan Nu,' said this lovely vision. 'In the sky I shall live forever, to be the guardian of silkworms here on earth. My festival will be the third day of the third month, when mulberry trees show their first green satin leaves. For my sake, let the young girls tend my silk-worms, calling them "little darlings". When the festival of Clear and Bright Weather comes, let the mulberry girls go out with their baskets, moving slowly through the orchards to fill them with glossy, dark leaves. Let them feed my silkworms faithfully, stay up to feed them all night, for they cannot go hungry even a quarter of an hour. If the late frosts come, turning green leaves to silver, let the farm boys light fires in the orchard to keep my darlings warm while they spin. Let the old man who sells charms in the market write spells to keep them from harm. Do all this faithfully, and in one month they will become snow-white thread, purer than jade, lovelier than crystal or waterfall – pure silk to delight you for ever.'

ANCIENT POPULAR LEGEND

Munch, munch, munch, munch –
My little lady among the leaves
Eating her dark green home. Yet, homeless, what
Households she hangs and furnishes!

4 · The dragon and his doctor

Long, long ago, in the days of the Yellow Emperor, lived a country-man called Huang. His home was in a remote place, where three or four farmhouses clustered round a horse-pond. The men of the hamlet ploughed, the boys minded the geese and ducks, the women and girls tended the gardens. Each farm had its horse in the stable, sheep or cow in the paddock, hens in the roost, doves on the roof-ridge, pigs snug in the sty and cat stretched out in the sun. Far off you could see hazy smoke rise from the roofs. Nearer at hand you might hear a dog bark somewhere in the lanes, a cock crow at the top of the mulberry tree or the girls gossip as they milked the cows. Anyone who was not happy in that place would never be happy at all.

All these country neighbours honoured Huang, for he was a wonderful doctor of sick animals. When the sheep coughed, or the cow would not calve or the piglets failed to thrive, they would run to fetch him. Then Huang would look at the sick beast intently, speak to it quietly and handle it gently with steady brown hands. He seemed to see through the illness to the nature of the creature itself, and the animals he treated with herbs or surgery were always healed. No wonder the farmers called him Dr Horse, in Chinese Dr Ma.

Ma was standing at the door one day, looking round his walled courtyard with its stables and barns, when a sudden shadow blotted out the sun. Slowly a flying dragon circled above the farm and glided down to land in front of him. Naturally Ma knew all about the dragons in theory, for the dragon was chief of the three-hundred and sixty scaly reptiles. He knew that four Dragon Kings rule the four seas, that the Celestial Dragon rules the sky, that the Earth Dragon marks out lakes and rivers, and that the Hidden Treasure Dragon guards the gold and silver deep in the earth. Dragons, he knew, were certainly magical. A foolish man once invented a recipe for cooking dragon-meat, but he never could catch one, so his skill was all wasted. The great Confucius himself said: *Birds fly, fishes swim and beasts run; you may snare those that run, hook those that swim and shoot those that fly. But when it comes to a dragon – he can ride on the wind and I can't imagine how to catch one.* Like everyone else, Ma also knew that a friendly dragon brings good luck and that is why people so often have them painted on dishes or screens. Yet, strangely enough, he had never seen one.

Now the dragon shuffled towards him on golden claws. Red, green and azure rippled through its golden scales from head to snaky tail, wreathing and dissolving into changing patterns with every breath. Yet the gorgeous dragon's head and tail hung slack, its ears drooped and from its open jaws a trail of spittle fell to the stones. Its topaz eyes gazed at him piteously.

'Why,' thought Ma in instant recognition, 'this dragon is ill and wants me to cure it!' Seeing only a suffering beast, he lost all sense of the fabulous monster. He examined it with a strong, delicate touch; searching the scaly temples, he felt the racing pulse of pain. The trouble was not hard to find, a red and angry abscess gathering on the jaw.

'Steady, old fellow,' said Ma, as though to a horse; and the dragon, hearing the authority in that quiet voice, stood trustingly under his hands. Ma fetched his case of acupuncture needles. Deftly, still talking calmly to the patient, he slid the fine gold and silver needles into the skin. After five minutes he withdrew them, so delicately that the dragon seemed to feel nothing.

Ma knew all the three-hundred and sixty-five points of the body at which a surgeon may practise this craft. 'Unhealthy fluids will drain away,' he explained reassuringly, 'the swelling will lessen, the healthy balance of the body will be restored and the pain will vanish.' Topaz eyes gazed at him, as though the dragon understood.

The dragon rested that night in his barn. Ma, in his still room, pounded liquorice root with pestle and mortar to make soothing medicine, which the dragon appeared to enjoy for it finished every drop and licked its chops. Next day Ma was satisfied to see the abscess draining, and the dragon resting comfortably, coiled in the straw. By the third morning it was cured, and flew away, rainbow scales glittering along the white fingers of the clouds, until it dwindled into the distance. Next day, it came back, with a pair of red jade slippers in its claws. Ma was deeply touched. 'Bless you, I want no reward,' he said. 'Jade slippers are not for the likes of me; nor any of your magic tricks like floating through the air or passing through solid rock. If you feel well, that's all the thanks I need.'

The dragon, like many human patients, was now deeply attached to its doctor. It went to live in the depths of the village pond, and every time it felt out of sorts appeared in Huang's courtyard like a persistent invalid at morning surgery. Ma knew what it wanted, and kept a jar always filled with the dragon's favourite dark, treacly liquorice medicine.

Of course, this strange friendship could not long remain unknown. A dragon is only a dragon, you might think, but foolish men can make it a god. Soon news spread through the land that a Holy Dragon lived in the village horse-pond. Happiness or grief, rain or drought, before long people were saying that it was all the dragon's doing. Crowds came on foot, nobles on horse-back and ladies in carrying chairs. They built a stone shrine beside the pool. They poured offerings of wine over the water-mint and burned sacrifices of sucking pig on the rocks; the foxes which came at night grew fat and drunk with finishing it all up. All day the crowds chanted prayers, waved silk umbrellas, threw paper money into the water or banged gongs and drums. Trippers from town trampled the barley fields, picked the flowers and frightened the hens until they stopped laying. No longer did the villagers stoop to see how their grain was growing, look up into their mulberry boughs or enjoy a friendly chat with the neighbours about the weather or crops. They were all too busy selling tea and rice-cakes to the tourists. Ma

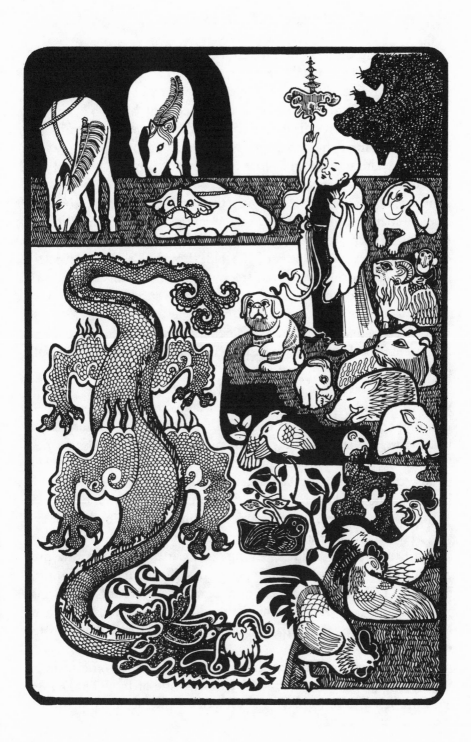

escaped to gather herbs in the calm shadows of the summer woods; yet even there loud picnic parties drove him away. 'It's as bad as a barbarian invasion,' he thought gloomily.

What did the dragon think of this incessant hubbub? Though worshippers implored it loudly, it refused to come out from its lair at the bottom of the pond, until one morning before sunrise Ma found it waiting at its old place in the yard. Bowing its head and spreading its great bat-wings, the dragon invited him to mount. No sooner had Ma swung a leg over the scaly golden back than the dragon soared into the clouds. They winged through the sky, red mists of morning wrapping them round like a cloak under the high canopy of space. The doors of the Jade Emperor's heavenly palace swung open and Ma wandered freely through the halls of the stars. Servants washed him in showers of rainbow spray, dressed him in silk robes and girded him with a belt of jewels, while the dragon vanished to the stables of the sky. Then they led Ma to the banqueting hall, to eat the Food of Long Life. Now his fame and glory would last for ever.

Like most men, Ma had expected one short life. 'The world is an inn,' he had said to himself, 'and we are passing travellers.' He was prepared to grow old, to find his hair and beard every day a little whiter, to lean each day a little more heavily on his thornwood stick, to drink a cup of wine in memory of friends gone before, and in his turn to meet the Common Change of death. 'By then,' he had said, 'the world and I will have had our fill of one another.'

Yet now that the dragon had carried him to the kingdom of the sky, Ma found everything quite unexpectedly usual. For there, every department of the Chinese Empire on earth has an everlasting counterpart. The Celestial Emperor has his court, his eighteen provinces with their governors, his judges, treasurers and mandarins, each with his host of attendant clerks, door-keepers and policemen. Naturally there is a celestial Ministry of Health, and the Minister soon sent for Ma.

'Welcome to our Ministry,' he said, with a polished official smile. 'I hereby appoint you to my staff, with the title of Infallible Dr Ma. Your duties will be to make a survey of all the medicinal plants on earth for the Office of Remedies. When you have completed it, kindly present your report to your senior officers, the Superintendent of the Celestial Pharmacy and the Eternal Apothecary.' Before Ma had time to open his mouth, a black-robed clerk bowed him out of the door.

So, as Infallible Dr Ma, he laboured many centuries collecting healing plants on earth, and planting a physic garden in the sky. There he grew, in neatly labelled flower beds, eight-hundred and ninety-eight vegetable drugs: peppermint and rhubarb for the stomach, horehound for coughs, wintergreen for sprains, witch hazel for bruises, lime-blossom for headache, vervein to calm the thoughts, balsam for wounds, soya beans for strength and poppy for sleep. For centuries to come, everyone in China swore by Dr Ma's infallible remedies. When this garden was finished, Ma received another appointment; to be the patron and protector of all the veterinary surgeons on earth. What an important job for a country horse doctor!

Indeed, Ma might have felt overwhelmed but for one faithful friend. Every so often the golden dragon would appear outside the Celestial Pharmacy and wait patiently, with drooping ears and appealing gaze. Ma did his best not to show how pleased he was to see it.

'There is really nothing the matter with you at all,' he said in as firm a voice as he could manage. Yet the dragon continued to look up in its peculiar manner, knowing that if it waited long enough, its favourite Dr Ma would pour it a dose of Heavenly Liquorice Medicine.

ANCIENT POPULAR LEGEND

> *Going on four feet*
> *Going on wings,*
> *The firm and gentle hand of the good healer*
> *Discovers no difference – all is life.*

5 · The great Yu

'Study hard,' said the old Chinese schoolmaster to his pupils. 'Work and do not spare yourselves, that you may become worthy servants of China, like the great Yu.'

'Venerable master,' said his favourite pupil, 'why is it that when a man spends his life in hard and disagreeable toil for others people say he is like the great Yu?'

'That is something every son of China should know,' answered the old schoolmaster; and taking an ivory comb from his sleeve he smoothed his long moustaches as he began to teach them.

'Long ago, when the Western barbarians lived in huts upon the hill tops and used knives of stone, our honourable ancestors in China lived already as we do today. They built cities on the banks of the Yellow River; they spoke the Chinese language and spun fine thread from the cocoon of the silkworm which fed upon their mulberry trees. Those were the days of ancient virtue; yet they were days of weeping too. For the Yellow River has another name.'

'It is called "China's Sorrow",' said the favourite pupil, and the old man nodded his head.

'In those days, long ago, the Yellow River brought sorrow indeed to China. High in the mountains it rises, a muddy torrent, foaming through the narrow valleys; it falls to the plains with a crash of thunder, and hungry, unresting, it eats its way for many leagues to the ocean. Even far out to sea, its yellow waters may still be seen, staining the blue of the ocean like a dye.

'In the days of which I speak, each year when the spring rains came, the river would burst its banks. Each year the waters covered more land. They swept away towns and villages; in the fields they drowned peasants at their work. When the waters rolled back, as far as the eye could see, a smooth lake of yellow mud spread over the land. No man could live there, only strange water birds, whose webbed feet made criss-cross patterns in the slime. As time passed, vast tangled forests grew up, where wild beasts roamed. Yes, those were days of sorrow indeed.' The old man stroked his moustaches and shook his head sadly.

'Yet in those days, in the safety of the hill country, lived a young man named Yu. He had been married only three days and he was seated with his bride in the courtyard of their new home, when a messenger, in the yellow robes of the Emperor's service, knocked at his gate.

' "Is this the house of Yu, son of Kwan?" demanded the messenger.

' "My name is Yu," replied the young man, "and this is my wife. We have been married these three days."

' "It grieves me, honourable Yu, to hear those words," said the messenger, "for I am the unworthy bearer of the Emperor's command. You must leave your bride and come with me. The Son of Heaven has read your plan for mastering the floods and he is pleased to appoint you Minister of the Yellow River."

'Yu's young wife wailed and hid her face in her hands; but, as Yu bowed his head in submission, his face was calm and even stern.

' "Farewell, my wife," he said. "I must obey the Son of Heaven's command. But when my work is done, then I will return to you. Remember – when my work is done!"

'Then Yu saddled his horse and rode with the messenger, whose name was Yih, to the city where the Emperor held his court.

'Yu's first task was to survey the great river along the whole of its course, from the mountain gorges where it rises, to the seven-channelled delta where its yellow waters pour into the sea. Through many provinces he followed it, while the blossoms fell and the fruit which ripened in their place was gathered into the farmers' winter

store. Beside Yu went his faithful friend and companion, the
messenger, Yih. They took boats out on to the swirling muddy
water, and measured the depth of the river with many lengths of
weighted cord; they tramped for days over the slimy mud of the
river bank; they rode on the hill tops, seeing the stretches of flood
and forest spread out below them like a map.

'The old year ended, a new year began; and once, as they climbed
a hill path, Yih looked down.

' "Honourable Yu," he said, "there, in the valley, I see a house,
a small house with a courtyard where a plum tree is in bloom.
Beneath the plum tree sits a young woman – I can see her dress of
red and green. She is rocking a cradle. Most honourable Yu, either
my eyes deceive me, or that house . . ."

' "Yes," said Yu, "I am looking at my own home. That is my
wife; and there, in the cradle, is my son. I can see from here how
the sunshine flashes on his little gold cap."

'But when Yih urged his friend to go home, even for a day, Yu
shook his head sternly and said, "Not until my work for China is
finished shall I return."

'Now, his survey completed, Yu was ready to carry out his plan
against the floods. He set armies of labourers to work digging out
the mud from the lower river-bed, and making a new, deep channel,
which would carry the headwaters safely to the sea. Huge gangs of
men toiled with shovels and buckets to haul up the yellow mud and
carry it far away from the river bank. When they met difficulties,
Yu himself was always there to help.

' "The men cannot reach the mid-channel to dig?" he would say.
"They must do as I did – take boats into mid-stream and drag up
the mud in buckets. . . . The men slip as they carry their load up
the slimy river bank, and fall back into the water to drown? They
must do as I did – drive spikes into the soles of their shoes to grip
the treacherous mud. . . . The men pushing wheelbarrows on the
shore sink to their knees in the slime? They must do as I did – tie
planks to their feet and pull sledges as though they were crossing
the snow. I tell you, all these things can be done, for this person
has done them all already!"

'While Yu toiled on the river bank, Yih burned down the great forests and led bands of huntsmen to trap the wild beasts. Then together they rode back into the hills.

' "Most honourable Yu," cried Yih, as their horses walked side by side, "we are passing your home once more. In the courtyard there is a boy – a fine sturdy boy of seven years it may be; he is galloping his wooden hobby-horse around the plum tree and beating it with a toy whip."

' "Yes," said Yu. "That is my son. When I have finished my work, I will return to him."

'The hardest part of Yu's work was still to come. Now he had to cut a new, wider channel for the upper reaches of the river, cutting through a spur of mountain called the Dragon Gate. The soil was hard like iron, full of solid rock. The labourers hacked with picks and shovels and wedges, inch by inch through the mountain-side. At last only one barrier of rock remained, against which the waves churned and frothed like hungry wolves.

'Yu stood by on the bank. "If I have reckoned wisely," he said, "the river will flow into its new deep channel and the banks will hold. If I have erred – then I am disgraced for ever, and there is nothing left for me but to die."

'He gave the signal; the workmen swung their picks all together, singing their endless monotonous working song, until the rocks began to topple, and suddenly, like a clap of thunder, the waters crashed through on their way to the valley below. For a moment nothing could be seen for clouds of spray; but Yu had cut the channel deep enough to hold the sudden avalanche of waters, which settled, swirling and bubbling between their banks in the valley below, and flowed safely on through the peaceful fields, out to the blue ocean.

'Now Yu went home at last, to the house with the little courtyard where the plum tree was once again in blossom. A tall, handsome young man, in scholar's gown of black, stood bowing before him, and tears filled the great Yu's eyes at the sight. "How tall you are, my son," he said. "You are almost as tall as your father."

'There was a knock at the outer gate. Yih the messenger stood once again outside.

' "This time you have not come to our lowly house to take him from us," said Yu's wife, smiling.

' "I have," said Yih. "But no, honoured Madam, do not look so sad. This is a joyful message which I bring. You know that our Emperor is old and that his eyes are growing dim; he wishes to rest in the years that remain to him. Honourable Yu, of all his servants, you have served most faithfully the Son of Heaven and he summons you to rule China in his stead." '

The old schoolmaster raised his white head and looked at the boys before him. 'You may go now; the lesson is ended,' he said. 'You may go to catch grasshoppers and play shuttlecock, since as yet you are only children. But remember. Study hard; work and do not spare yourselves, so that one day you may become worthy servants of China – like the great Yu.'

TWENTY-SECOND CENTURY B.C.

Many years of labour with the world's business;
A few months of play with wife and child.
Which is life, the task or the holiday?
Can a great person also be a man?

6 · Tzu Chu's cheerful funeral

When the rich merchant Tzu Chu died, his young wife was appalled. Not that she missed him; he had been a grumpy, disagreeable old man and, to speak frankly, no one would miss him very much. But in those far-off days, custom demanded that the living wife should be buried in the dead husband's grave. His slaves would also be buried, and even now she could hear them howling in their quarters. Yet they were only slaves, she thought resentfully, and what else could they expect? But for herself; never again to see the fountain's glittering plume, never to lie in bed sipping tea on rainy autumn mornings! Like a great wheel her heart turned in her breast and she shuddered deeper into her furs.

She had always known what must come, from childhood, when she saw her brothers gallop on bamboo hobby-horses, wear red shoes and embroidered coats and bellow if they did not get their own way. Yet she had to sleep on the floor, wear cotton clothes, cook, sew and weep in silence, the wooden pillow wet with her tears. 'No one is glad when a girl is born,' she thought bitterly, 'and no one will cry when I am in my grave, my husband's grave.'

Now along came her husband's confidential clerk, black-robed and obsequious, with his usual list of notes on a bamboo tablet. 'You need not have the slightest anxiety, madam,' he said smoothly. 'All arrangements for the funeral of my lamented master and your husband, Tzu Chu, are well in hand. His horses, hounds, carriage and slaves will, of course, be buried with him, since he might need them in the Nether World. Jade has naturally been placed in his mouth to preserve his body.' Though to himself he thought, that all it will do is to make tomb-robbers rich! He did not say this aloud but continued with his list. 'Mourning-garments have been ordered, strictly white, of course, with rice gruel for the household to eat and floor-mats to sleep on during the month of mourning.'

'The mourners?' she asked faintly.

'Naturally we have engaged professional mourners of the highest standing. They are guaranteed to speak only of deaths and burials for a full month, and also to stamp the earth, beat their breasts and wail loudly, enough to keep away the most determined demons.'

He smiled, with hateful smugness, and a brilliant idea struck the little widow.

'Tzu Chu always spoke so highly of you,' she said persuasively. 'I am sure nothing would give him more satisfaction than for you to go down into the grave with him, and attend upon him at the Yellow Springs.'

'Madam, you do me too much honour!' cried the clerk in great haste. To go deep down beneath the Yellow Springs, he thought, to lie thousands of years without waking, in the long dark night that hold the dead – all this for old fusspot, his fault-finding employer – no, thank you! 'The dead are gone and with them we cannot converse,' he said, 'yet I feel sure my beloved master would prefer *your* company.'

For a while they kept silence, eyeing one another narrowly. Then the clerk made a suggestion. 'Tzu Chu had a brother, Tzu Heng.'

'So I have heard,' said the widow. 'He declined to enter the family business establishment and retired to a pavilion in a bamboo thicket, where he passes his time reading books.'

'Then he will surely have read what the sages say, that of all men living, none is so close as a brother,' said the clerk swiftly. 'If so insignificant a person may venture to offer advice, I suggest, madam, that we should send a runner with an invitation to Tzu Heng.'

The day of the funeral came and Tzu Heng appeared. He was a white-haired scholar of vaguely distinguished, but shabby, appearance. When the clerk set a bowl of green tea at his elbow, Tzu Heng bowed his thanks but forgot to drink it.

'Your brother, Tzu Chu, requires someone of the highest excellence to attend upon him at the Yellow Springs,' said Madam Tzu. 'So we must ask you kindly to go down with his body into the grave. We are quite sure that there is no one he would rather have.'

'Respect for ceremony binds the whole human race. Yet if it is a question of attendance,' said the scholar, 'I fear I should prove a lamentably inefficient housekeeper, in this world or the next. However, who better suited to attend on my dear brother than his wife? And, of course,' he added as an afterthought, 'his indispensable secretary.' He bowed politely to the clerk, who set his teeth and bowed silently in return.

Tzu Heng regarded them both gravely for a while. 'Yet do we know,' he said, 'that burial of the living with the dead is really necessary? This is an interesting question.'

'How can you be so calm?' cried the widow.

'When my brother died,' said the scholar, 'I was in despair, as any man might be. Yet soon I saw that death is part of life. We receive life because the time has come; we lay it down for the same reason. If we praise life, surely we must praise death also – once a man has understood that, he is beyond grief or joy.'

'But the prescribed mourning . . .' began the widow.

The scholar held up one papery old hand. 'When someone is tired and has gone to lie down, do we break in on his rest with bawling and stamping? Tzu Chu, whom we have lost, has lain down to sleep in the Great Inner Room. Should we break in on his rest in an unmannerly fashion?'

They wanted to believe him, yet custom held them fast. 'Suppose,' said the clerk nervously, 'Tzu Chu's spirit should refuse to take up residence in its tablet in the Hall of the Ancestors and return to haunt us?' He shuddered; he had always been frightened of ghosts.

'The great Confucius did not believe in ghosts,' continued the scholar calmly. 'For just as there is no smoke without a fire, how can there be a spirit without a body to live in? Why display chariots and jade, why bury men and women and fill the air with ceaseless wailing when death is the natural end of every living thing? The whole matter will be obvious to distinguished intellects such as yours.' He permitted himself a frosty smile.

'Then what would your Learned Excellency propose?' they asked at last.

'Let us have decent lamentations for three days,' said the sage, 'then take off our mourning garments and enjoy a good meal, for at a banquet the soul puts forth flowers.'

'But the women of the household . . .' cried the widow.

'Let them all, fine ladies or serving maids, go safely back to their own homes.'

Little Madam Tzu gazed at him as though she had seen the red sun rise twice in one morning. Yet she could not quite shake off the dread of a lifetime.

'Forgive a woman's foolish fears, Great Sage, yet there must surely be *something* which the dead demand of us?'

'To show respect for honourable ancestors,' said the scholar consideringly, 'let the invited guests send money, slaves, horses, chariots and clothes made out of paper for the dead person to use at the Yellow Springs. Those who wish to display their wealth might make such trifles out of parcel-gold or jade, while the living are spared to live out their span here on earth.'

'An excellent idea!' cried the clerk hastily. 'This humble person will take it upon himself to draw up a list of guests immediately!'

'Meanwhile,' continued the philosopher, 'though many take drugs to achieve long life, better far to drink good wine with a quiet mind.'

The clerk crooked one finger to order the house-slaves, who, scarcely able to believe their good fortune, were already lighting the charcoal under the square, bronze wine-warmer. Soon brother, wife and confidential clerk raised their gently-steaming goblets and drank a toast: 'To the cheerful funeral of Tzu Chu!'

SIXTH CENTURY B.C.

Custom is a collar
Clamps our neck, criminals.
Comes a man of piercing sense,
Guilt falls off in freedom.

7 · Heartless beauty

The young queen, Lustrous Tortoiseshell, wife of the last king of the house of Chou, had eyes the colour of topaz. Her skin was as smooth as her petticoat of apricot-yellow satin, and when she yawned she showed the inside of a mouth as coral and crinkled as a cat's. She yawned often, for she found life in the palace remarkably tedious. Indeed, the king was a dull, gloomy man whose courtiers would hide their smiles behind their wide sleeves when they saw him coming, for fear of incurring his displeasure.

It was not altogether the king's fault. Ever since he had ascended the Dragon Throne, the borders of China had been menaced by enemy horsemen, and every day he was forced to spend long hours in council with his ministers discussing their defence, until his forehead was furrowed with care. But Lustrous Tortoiseshell did not understand this, and instead of seeking humbly to please her lord, or to distract his mind from care – which all the ancient writings agree is the first duty of a wife – she preferred to sulk in her own apartments. Bored, she tore up pieces of valuable silk, her eyes glinting with pleasure at the sound. The rasp of rending embroideries set the king's teeth on edge and made him gloomier than ever.

'Lustrous Tortoiseshell,' he implored her, 'the King of Chou is your slave, but he begs you humbly not to tear up any more silk.'

For answer the queen only yawned and tapped impatiently with her little foot upon the floor. The king sent for jugglers, lute players and dancing bears; he ordered merchants to bring their most precious wares of jade and ivory and chiselled gold, yet still this spoilt beauty continued to frown. He was in despair to know how to please her.

At last one day, when Lustrous Tortoiseshell had sat sulking for two hours without a smile, the king had an idea. He gathered up his long robe, took a lighted taper in his hand, and climbed the winding stair to the highest watch-tower of the palace, where a sentry stood night and day looking out over the plain. There upon the floor a great fire was prepared: brushwood, pine-cones and logs of cedar-wood, all ready to flare up at a touch. It was the beacon to give warning that the enemy was at hand. Into this beacon the king thrust his lighted taper.

There was a rustle among the twigs, a sudden roar, and flames leaped like a fountain into the air. Soon, almost at once it seemed, came an answering roar from the distance. It was the sound of many hands beating on bronze war drums, as the faithful nobles of Chou led their troops out of their castles to defend the king. Winding down the valleys they came, from each castle an army of men, on horse, on foot, with banners streaming in the wind, forests of lances glittering in the sunshine, and chariots swaying from side to side in their headlong advance.

Lustrous Tortoiseshell, all boredom forgotten, watched from her window as the armies met and poured in like a mighty river at the city gate. They crowded into the courtyard of the palace, jostling for position and shouting their battle-cries. Some of the foot-soldiers, in the belief that the enemy was at hand, began to throw their firecrackers without waiting for orders, and so terrified the horses that several onlookers were trampled to death

The chief nobles of Chou rode forward to the palace doors upon their foaming chargers. They were accoutred for war, their supple leather riding-boots pulled up to their thighs, their well-flighted arrows in quivers at their sides, the vizors of their bronze helmets, grim and terrible, pulled over their eyes. They reined in their horses and waited silently at the palace steps for their king to come out and lead them.

But the King of Chou was too ashamed to show his face. In an inner courtyard of the palace he gave himself over to despair.

'Honoured sirs, honoured sirs,' called Lustrous Tortoiseshell from the window, 'you may all go home to your castles of exalted virtue, and there employ the remainder of your days peacefully flying kites. The enemy is not here.'

'Not here?'

'Not here?'

Spurs and bridle bells clashed together as the nobles turned to look at each other.

'But the beacon?'

'We saw the beacon flames!'

'The Son of Heaven called us to defend him!'

'His Majesty was pleased to jest with you,' said Lustrous Tortoiseshell.

Silently, without reproach, so great was their love and loyalty, the nobles turned away. But Lustrous Tortoiseshell, when she saw their amazement, their sorrowful looks, and all their warlike trappings hanging useless at their sides, began to laugh.

She flung back her head, closed her eyes narrowly, and laughed and laughed for joy, until the last soldier, weary and crest-fallen, had left the city gates on his homeward journey. Then she went to the king.

'At last, O King of Chou,' she cried, 'at last you have found means to amuse your wife! How foolish their faces looked when they found there was no enemy! O my husband, what a splendid pastime you have invented!'

Shame struck the King of Chou afresh at these words of an idle and worthless woman. At the council table he could hardly bear to meet the grave looks of his ministers, and he vowed that he would never deceive his faithful lords again. But the weeks passed and Lustrous Tortoiseshell grew bored once more. She wheedled and cajoled the unhappy king, she tormented him with her caprices, until in despair he set fire once again to the beacon.

This time the nobles of Chou obeyed the summons with dark looks, and when they saw there was no enemy, departed murmuring

that even the king ought not so to make fools of them. When this unwise ruler lit the beacon yet a third time, the nobles chose one, the oldest and most honourable of their numbers, to plead with him. The aged lord, white-haired and venerable, prostrated himself humbly upon the steps of the throne.

'Son of Heaven, ruler of Earth and Sea,' he said. 'Hear, we pray you, the petition of your servants. We know your every thought is for your people's good. Nevertheless there are, around the Dragon Throne, evil counsellors whose actions, if you but knew of them, your Majesty would never permit. It would be well, O Son of Heaven, if these persons were sent into some distant and unwholesome province. For upon the honour of our ancestors, we nobles of Chou will not be mocked again.'

'I give you my royal word,' said the king, 'that I will never again light the beacon to mock you. Go in peace.' And, laden with rich gifts, he sent them to their homes.

The very next day, as the king and Lustrous Tortoiseshell sat at rice, the watcher on the tower came running down the winding stair and flung himself in terror at their feet.

'Son of Heaven, the enemy is coming!' he cried.

'Where?' said the king, thrusting the golden goblet from his hand.

'Down the mountain-sides, through the valleys – their grey cloaks are sweeping like mist over the plain!'

'Let the beacon be lit!' commanded the king. 'Have no fear, my beautiful Lustrous Tortoiseshell, my nobles will bring their armies to defend me.'

But although they fed the beacon fire until its flames leaped high as a tall tree, although they beat the bronze war drums and all the temple gongs, yet the nobles did not come. They remembered the laughter of Lustrous Tortoiseshell and feared to be mocked once more.

Then the King of Chou saw – but too late – where his weakness and folly had brought him. As the thunder of enemy horse-hoofs sounded nearer and nearer across the plain, he took Lustrous Tortoiseshell by the hand and led her to the tower. When they were both inside he commanded his servants to lock the doors and heap brushwood all around. With his own hands he set fire to the silken hangings. As the first barbarian entered the city gates the king and Lustrous Tortoiseshell perished, both together, in the flames.

So ended the House of Chou.

THIRD CENTURY B.C.

Nothing is gained, all is lost
Where Heartless Beauty lives.
The man who marries one of these
Has witnessed his own death-warrant.

8 · The broken lute-string

Hear now a tale of friendship. In the early days of the Chou dynasty there lived a famous man, a minister at court, whose name was Po-Ya. This Po-Ya had been on an embassy to a nearby state, and now, having exchanged gifts of gold and coloured satin, he was returning by river, in a great junk with carved oars.

It was autumn, the time of the harvest moon. Po-Ya had nothing to do; his mind was tranquil and he spent the time sitting on deck under an awning, playing music upon his seven-stringed lute, while the peaceful countryside slid by on either bank. But on these broad waters storms suddenly arise, especially in the autumn; and on the night of the mid-autumn festival a fierce storm of wind and rain overtook Po-Ya's ship. The sailors steered for the shore and moored at a bend in the river, just below a wooded cliff. Then, as suddenly as it had come, the storm cleared. The full moon hung like a silver wheel in the sky, shining upon the dark headland and the smooth water, and Po-Ya's thoughts were filled with music at the sight.

'Bring my lute on the deck,' he commanded. 'Place it before me, and light the sticks of sweetly smelling wood in the bronze bowl, for I wish to play.'

The servant bore the lute respectfully to his master, and Po-Ya tuned it, while delicate wreaths of smoke from the scented sticks floated up in the moonlight. Then he shook back the sleeves of his long silk robe and began to play. But he had not played for long when suddenly, beneath his fingers – *twang* – a broken string!

Po-Ya was startled. 'If we had been near a city,' he said, 'I should have said some scholar was listening to my playing, for it is well known that the presence of a person who understands the lute may often cause a string to break. But here, in this wild place, who could it be?'

Suddenly, to his amazement, Po-Ya heard a voice answer him from the shore. 'It is I who was listening, I, a poor woodcutter sheltering from the storm, who heard your beautiful music.'

'What?' said Po-Ya to himself. 'A woodcutter among the mountains who understands how well I was playing the lute? I do not believe it; this is some educated person who has disguised himself to spy on me. Come aboard, honourable sir!' he called. 'Come aboard and show yourself!'

But when the stranger stepped across the plank, Po-Ya's servant was astonished to see that he really was a woodcutter. No one could have invented a disguise so ragged and miserable. On his head he wore a broad hat of bamboo leaves, over his shoulders a cloak of long grasses; in his belt was stuck a woodcutter's chopper, and his muddy feet were half covered by broken sandals made of rushes.

Po-Ya's servant was shocked by his appearance. 'My good fellow,' he said, 'you really cannot appear before my master looking like that. Why, he is the famous Po-Ya, a minister at court, a great lord!'

'He is also a great lute player,' replied the woodcutter, 'and for that, I assure you, I shall show him respect.' So saying, he took off his hat and raincloak and carefully wiped the mud off his sandals before he entered the cabin where Po-Ya was sitting in the candle-light at a table, tuning the new string he had just put in his lute.

'My worthy man,' said Po-Ya haughtily, 'we will not stand on ceremony.' He waved his hand to his servant to set a stool for the stranger as far away as possible. 'So it was you who was listening on the river bank to my lute?' he continued.

'Yes, your Excellency,' replied the woodcutter, 'and, if one may say so, enjoying the masterly touch with which you were playing it.'

'Indeed!' said Po-Ya, taken aback. 'Then since you are so well acquainted with the principles of music, you will not mind if I put your knowledge to the test.'

'I should like it, if you please,' said the woodcutter with a smile.

Po-Ya frowned. 'Perhaps you are not aware that if one thinks of a certain thing when playing the lute, an educated listener will be able to read one's thoughts from the music?'

'Indeed, yes,' said the woodcutter, still smiling, 'that is written in the Book of Songs. There is a poem about it.'

'Hm! Poetry as well!' said Po-Ya. 'But then any ignorant person could pick up a poem without really understanding it. Now, pray listen to what I am about to play, and tell me what is in my mind.'

He played great rolling chords on the lower strings, then paused, expecting to see the woodcutter dumbfounded and ashamed.

'Beautiful!' said the woodcutter in admiration. 'Your Excellency was thinking of the rushing waters of a mighty river.'

'What!' exclaimed Po-Ya. 'Indeed, yes, I was. Oh but after all, since we are moored by a river bank, any ignorant person might have guessed that. Pray listen once more.'

He played rapid cascades and flurries of notes on the higher strings.

'Stop!' cried the woodcutter after a few bars. 'Let me tell you. Your Excellency was thinking of your summer palace, high in the mountains. The snow begins to melt and the tinkling streams fall down the mountain-side, leaping from stone to stone in the bright sunlight.'

Po-Ya pushed the lute away, stood up, and bowed to the stranger. 'I have been grievously lacking in courtesy towards a scholar and a master musician. Truly within this rough stone there lies a vein of perfect jade. May I ask your honourable name?'

'My name is Chung Hsi,' replied the woodcutter. 'I live in the village nearby and labour all day as a woodcutter to support my old parents; but at night I study all that I can find in books – music, poetry, history and the laws. A man may be poor, but he can always learn if he has the will.'

'I see you are a good son as well as a wise scholar,' said Po-Ya. 'Tonight we shall drink together and swear to be as brothers.'

'But, your Excellency, you are a great lord, and I, I am only. . . .'

'Music makes all who understand it brothers,' answered Po-Ya, and summoning his servant he ordered him to bring tea and mulled wine and to light the candles on the table of ceremony.

So all night Po-Ya, the great lord, and Chung Hsi, the poor woodcutter, stayed up together, pouring wine for each other and talking and playing the lute. They agreed to return and meet by the river's edge at exactly the same time the following year. In the morning, while the sailors lowered the gang-plank, Po-Ya gave his friend two small bars of gold to buy books for his studies, and accompanied him to the prow of the ship. There they parted in tears and Po-Ya sailed away.

The following year, when the festival of mid-autumn came round, Po-Ya returned to the lonely headland to keep his promise. Once more it was late evening, but in the clear moonlight it was as light as day. While the sweet-smelling smoke curled upwards Po-Ya sat in the stern of the boat and played the lute to call his friend, the woodcutter, Chung Hsi. He played a joyful tune, for his heart was cheerful at the thought of their meeting; but hardly had he begun to play, when one of the strings slipped between his fingers with a mournful sound.

'What does this mean?' Po-Ya asked himself in alarm. 'Can some evil have befallen my friend Chung Hsi? Why is he not here to meet me as he promised? I must find him.'

The gangway was lowered and Po-Ya went on shore. He was so anxious that he was still holding his lute as he made his way through the woods and the rocks, searching for the village where Chung Hsi lived. Dawn came and he had not yet found it; but on the bare hillside he saw an old man coming towards him, an old peasant with a bamboo hat and white hair.

'Old man!' called Po-Ya, and the peasant bowed respectfully.

'Is your Excellency looking for anything?' he asked.

'Yes. I am looking for a villager, a woodcutter by the name of Chung Hsi . . .' Po Ya broke off in amazement, for the old man's eyes had filled with tears.

'Chung Hsi! He was my son!' he cried.

'Was? Then he is. . . .'

'He is dead,' said the old man. 'Oh, your Excellency, it is a strange story. Last autumn, at the time of the full moon, he was coming home late from his woodcutting, when he met a great lord whose name was Po-Ya. They talked the whole night through – about music, I believe – and this great lord promised to be as a brother to my son. Before he sailed away, he gave him gold bars to help with his studies. With these Chung Hsi bought books, alas, many books. Every day he worked so hard for my wife and myself, every night he studied so hard at these books, that his strength failed. He lies buried in the hillside above us here. But, your Excellency – you are weeping too at this tale of a poor man's son!'

'I am weeping for my dear brother,' said the minister. 'My name is Po-Ya.'

Hand in hand they climbed to the granite stones where Chung Hsi was buried. The peasants, going out to work in the fields, saw the great lord in his robes going to the wayside grave, and followed to watch. Po-Ya stood in silence by the grave. Then he said, 'Chung Hsi, my friend! You who understood the lute so well – now I shall see if you can understand even when you are dead.'

And as one of the peasants brought forward a bronze bowl and lit the sticks of sweetly scented wood, Po-Ya played the lute by Chung Hsi's grave. Suddenly he stopped, and taking a dagger from his sleeve slashed it across the strings. Then, raising the lute he hurled it down on the sharp stones, smashing the polished wood and scattering the pegs of jade.

'Chung Hsi!' he cried. 'Since none but you understood my music, so now for your sake I shall play on this lute no more. Farewell, my friend Chung Hsi, farewell!'

THIRD CENTURY B.C.

The thoughts that others think,
Being with music blended,
I know within my heart
Just what the notes intended.
But when a friend is dead
All thought is out of tune.
Silent the lute, and dumb
The silver-echoing moon.

9 · How the Great Wall was built

Do you see those two old beggarmen, sitting on the ground? Always they sit there – filthy rags and bare feet, heads covered with dust, twice ten fingers black, hands gnarled as boots, legs and arms twisted, crutches to walk, eyes sunken and bleared, no teeth in their heads – two old men turned the colour of smoke. They have no friends, no family, no home. Their bodies might have died far away, and their ghosts hovered by bones there was no son to bury. For these two men were taken to build the Great Wall. Ask them and they will tell you their tale, first one and then the other, speaking in cracked, hoarse voices.

'We were young men of Chin, the land of the Dragon. Our home was called the Middle Kingdom, for we knew it was the middle of the world.'

'Then we were young and strong; now we are as you see us. Young years how few! Age how bitter! Yet we are alive when all the rest are dead.'

'Each morning we took a hoe and trudged out to work. Few acres, but our own, and the summer nights were worth a thousand pieces of gold!'

They look back at the past and sigh; then they take up their story.

'Came a new Emperor. What was that to us in our village?'

'He made a tour of the land and he said, "I will be the First Emperor of all China." So he made districts with governors and stern laws. Everywhere the same coins, the same weights and measures; everywhere the same roads, where fifty men could walk abreast. What was that to us? We had no mind to leave home.'

'Then he said, "I will not allow a hundred ways of thinking and writing. All ways must be one – my way!" So he made a law that all bamboo tablets with writing must be burned on a huge bonfire. All those who would not give up their old writings were branded with red-hot iron. But what was that to us, who could neither read nor write?'

'They say the First Emperor dug a Marvellous Canal, where ships could come and go between the two great rivers. They say he built a Palace City, roofed roads, a hall for ten thousand, pagodas, bells, drums and beautiful women. But we have never seen any of this.'

'They say the Emperor read a hundred and twenty pounds weight of words each day and that he went about in disguise to spy out his enemies. When he caught them he put them in prison till the skies rain wheat and horses grow horns, and this we believe.'

'So, cracking his whip, the Emperor swallowed up the land and overthrew the old lords; they bowed their heads and pleaded for their lives. He ruled in six directions at once and shook the four seas; the First Emperor was master of the world. All we wanted was to live in peace on our farms – but it was not to be!'

The two aged beggars groan and tears run down their furrowed cheeks at the knowledge of what was to come.

'Then the Emperor said, "I will join all the walls in the north to make one Great Wall of China; outside the wall all are barbarians, within the wall all are brothers. Take the strongest young men from every village in China. They are the ones to build my wall!"'

'So they came to our village to take us. Throughout the village was weeping and wailing; fathers must leave their children, husbands part from their wives. We were sent away and did not know if we should ever return, so bitter was our fate.'

'Long, long was the road to the north and the journeying hard. The pathway ran between cliffs, where red mountains glared at us. There were poisonous black serpents; in the desert scorpions shot their poison, in the swamp flying insects stung us. At the foul ponds many died of poison and the living trampled over the dead.'

'When we got to the northern frontier, the winters brought thick snow. We toiled, our hair and beards turned to icicles, our padded jackets iron with frost, while the shrieking wind drowned our groans. Much grieving and little sleeping, our dreams were all of home. To hear a song of the old country would pierce us to the heart.'

'To mark out the line of the wall, the Emperor ordered his own horse to be saddled; then he whipped it up and let it wander free. The horse snorted and cantered across the desert, over hills and mountains, through ravines and valleys for fifteen-hundred miles. It ran from the sea in the east to the westernmost border of China, and the architects struggled after it, sticking pegs in the track of its hooves.'

'Wherever the horse had trod and the pegs were set, we workmen had to build. The Great Wall was in truth two walls, the space between them wide enough to drive a war-chariot and packed solid with rocks and stones. Wherever the horse stamped they put a pole with a flag. There we had to build a square watch-tower, with lookout windows on each side, from which sentry could call to sentry along the whole length of the Wall. Between the towers, brick by brick, we laid battlements, breast high. Not a distant camp fire by night, nor a moving cloud of travellers' dust by day, not the sound of voices or the far-off blast of a Tartar horn would escape the ears of the sentries. To guard China, we labourers were forced to build fifteen-thousand towers; outside the wall we dug ditches and moats, inside we made camps for the frontier armies.'

'Many, many, the tales of the Great Wall, though now only we are left to tell them, remembering those days. The roll-call each waking, the march from the camp before dawn, the bowl of soup at noon, now thin, now bitter its taste! How can we forget those years?'

'The Emperor saddled his horse and now he rode up and down, swift as the wind from camp to camp. Men like to tell a tale that he carried a magic horse-whip. With one wave of this whip, so they tell you, the Emperor cut a pathway through mountains, or dug a new channel in the earth to turn the Yellow River out of its course. Things did not happen so quickly, though. The earth was dug with spades and carried in baskets, and the mountains moved by the miner's axe, blow by blow, stone by stone. The Emperor stood by on his tall horse, watching. Perhaps his whip was magic, but we felt its weight on our backs!'

'Then a rumour swept through all the camps, to make our blood run cold. The Emperor said, "I must kill a million men and bury them in the Wall. Then a million ghosts will guard it for ever and the barbarians from the north can never break through." That day we were almost dead men; we had lost all hope for our lives. But the architects begged the Emperor, lying flat on their faces before him, saying, "How can we build the Great Wall of China, when all our workmen are dead?" Then they found a wretched man in the camps, whose name was the character for Million. They dragged him before the Emperor, howling and pleading for his life, though he knew his end had come. The Emperor gave the sign with his black fan; miserable Million was cut down. We built his dead body into the Wall, and the work went on as before.'

'Sixteen years passed, weary and hungry both, through heavy days and nights. Hard in the heat when the sun glared down on us, sad in the rain when yellow dusk thickened, bitter in winter when the wind shrank the flesh on our bones. Our bodies, once young and strong, were covered with gashes and sores. A single hod of stone – how heavy it weighs!'

'We were watched all day at the Wall, for the Emperor had his spy. This was his terrible dog, different by day or by night. In the day the dog was red, like the earth; in the night it was black, like the dark. This dog had a marvellous nose; it could smell out bad workmen. If a First Hand Worker took wood to burn on his camp-fire at night, Black Dog would smell him and bark to the store-keeper. This dog had long, sharp ears which could hear many miles away and knew the speech of all lands. Not a plot to run away, nor a plan to rest escaped it. Wherever men work or build, the Drinking Tea Rest is lawful. Yet Red Dog prowled the Wall, and

when it caught us resting it would bark to its masters. Then the guards came with sticks and whips and drove us back to work. The hours of toil were long, so long that men slept where they stood. If they fell in the sand they were buried, and never woke up again. All this Red Dog watched with eyes as hard as stones. Then it made its report to its master, wagging its tail in signals, and all who had slept were punished. You may think this story is strange, but how else did the Emperor know?'

'Those that were punished were driven in chains, so weak they could hardly stand. Even the horses staggered beneath their loads, and the cart oxen sweated under the yoke. The men who died lie in long, long rows, mounds and graves where white bones are heaped. No one knows who they are; no word can they speak, nor can they know when spring has come. The Great Wall is their grave.'

Sadly, bitterly, they come to the end of their story.

'At last the Wall was built. When it was done, they filled the towers with bowmen who did not miss their mark. Officers seized and questioned all who went in or out at the gates. The sand dunes were filled with soldiers' tents and the generals kept a tiger tally to number each man.'

'No chance to desert; a soldier might serve his whole life at the Great Wall, while at home his wife wandered in dreams through desert sands, or wept useless tears alone. It is a sorrow the women could hardly bear.'

'Then the First Emperor said to himself: "With my strong city, my laws, my walls of iron stretching a thousand miles, I have made an Empire which my children's children will keep for ten-thousand generations." '

'So the Great Wall was built, but the Emperor died the common death of all men.'

'Yet the Wall still stands.'

'And what of us who built it?'

The two old men speak in chorus, holding out their grimy hands to beg for alms.

'We wander half-starved through the streets of the city. The fire of grief has burnt out our hearts. Those that are gone we shall not see again, and of where they lie no one can give us news. A handful of rice each day, that is all we have left to live for. For we are alive when all the rest are dead.'

So the two old men spoke and I cannot forget their words.

THIRD CENTURY B.C.

Blocks of stone high to every horizon.
Climbing close they dribble a fine mortar.
What is the dry white powder holds them together?
The cracked bone and chalk marrow of men.

10 · Hsiang Yu's last battle

In the days of the First Emperor, bookburner and wallbuilder, China was great. Outside on the lonely plains, barbarians lived in black tents, drove their sheep, drank mare's milk and rested on the ground. Within the Great Wall, the Chinese slept in beds, sat on chairs, addressed each other with courtly politeness, wrote and painted on scrolls, made music or played games of chess. Yet for all this they paid a heavy price. To every little kingdom in the Empire, the black-robed tax collector came each year; all that a man could earn by farming or a woman by silk-spinning would hardly fill his account scrolls. Moreover, every kingdom had to send soldiers to the Emperor's army. Sometimes a peasant would take a heavy stone and break his own right arm; better to live in pain a lifelong cripple than be fighting at the Wall, a thousand miles from home. And each year, new ghosts waited with the old.

Then the First Emperor died, and before three years were out the kingdom rose against his weak and foolish son. In the wars that followed, palaces and houses were burned to ashes, walls left broken and gaping, while the Emperor's capital smouldered for three months. Fragments of beaten armies looted their way across the land like plagues of locusts. Hazy the smoke rose from ruined villages. With husbands dead, wives dragged the plough or fields grew choked with weeds and could never be ploughed again. No man was at peace. Even the scholar took off his purple sash, put on a jerkin of rhinoceros hide, rolled up his skirts and shouldered a bow until he too died. Dead soldiers were food for crows and their horses wandered riderless. In the morning men went out to battle and in the evening they did not return. Blood flowed like the sea. Soon a new House of Emperors, the Han, would arise. Yet there would still be generals loyal to the old ruler. The bravest of these was Hsiang Yu. Hear now the story of his last battle.

Hsiang Yu was a plain and simple man, content to eat and drink the same things as the common soldiers. When on the march they came to water, he would not go near it until all his men had finished drinking, nor would he eat till they had all been fed. Likewise he would not rest until the famous white charger Silver, which he always rode, had been stabled. Knowing this, the soldiers loved Yu and served him faithfully.

The soldiers had fought long and hard against the Emperor's enemies; few were left and their supplies were running out, so they built a stockade to rest.

Sentry called to sentry through the long chill nights, or beat out the hours on an empty copper pot. Nights were uneasy with the clank of arms, the stamp of hooves, the neighing of a restless horse; each man grasped his sword, feeling it icy to his touch. Then one night came the far-off blast of a horn and the tramp of marching men. The Han armies had surrounded them. In the darkness, Hsiang Yu heard them, all around his camp, singing the songs of many kingdoms. 'How many nations they have with them!' he exclaimed. 'Has Han already conquered all China?' Then he got up in the night, and drank within the curtains of his tent. Filled with passionate sorrow he began to sing, composing this song:

> *My strength pulled up mountains,*
> *My shadow darkened the world.*
> *But the times have turned against me;*
> *Silver will run no more.*

Tears of grief streamed down Yu's face, yet his heart was high. He mounted Silver, rallied eight-hundred brave knights, burst through the enemy lines under his White Tiger banner and galloped away to the south. Daylight came and Ying, the Han general, saw they had escaped him. He set off in pursuit with five-thousand troops; war chariots rattled and men-at-arms marched with swinging stride, while all about them red dust swirled shoulder high.

Meanwhile Hsiang Yu had forded a river and lost his way among lonely dykes and dunes. 'Which way to firm ground?' he shouted to an old farmer, who was planting rice shoots in the mud.

'Go left,' said the old man with a grin.

But the farmer deceived them, for the left took them deeper and deeper into a swamp. Frightened horses plunged in the mud, chariots sank axle-deep, men weighted with armour and heavy clubs were sucked down to their death. When Yu, on Silver, at last struggled to dry land, he had only twenty-eight horsemen, and sweeping in from the right thundered the Han cavalry.

Then Yu said to himself, 'Let me depart, for my time has run out.' He put on his bronze helmet, his breastplate of hide, his black bow curved like the young moon, his sword of cold iron. Turning he addressed the remnant of his army. 'In my time I have fought seventy battles, and never once was I defeated. Yet now I am brought to ruin, for Fate means to destroy me. I have made up my mind to die today, but before I go I will win you three victories. For your sake I will breach the enemy line, cut down their leaders and capture their banners. So you may see it is Fate, not my own weakness, which destroys me.'

Then Yu drew up his horsemen in a hollow square around a hill top to await the enemy. The Han horde rolled on, spears flashing, chariots wheel to wheel, flags and banners flapping against the sky, jade sticks beating a war-song on the drums. When they came near, Yu said to his horsemen: 'I will get one of those generals for you. When I shout the order, ride against the enemy, and re-group on the east side of the hill.'

Reining in Silver, Yu watched and waited. Then he shouted, 'Charge!' and thundered down the hill. He roared and glared so fiercely that the Han troops scattered before him like frightened hens. Hacking his way through them, he cut down a Han general and swerved to rejoin his own men. There at the east of the hill they re-grouped, grimed, blood-splashed and in rags, while Han

squadrons circled uneasily round them, not knowing which in this band of desperate men was General Yu.

Then Yu again set Silver to the charge. Whirling his sword he cut through the ranks of Han, killing fifty men and snatching their standard. When he gathered his horsemen again, he found that in all this fighting he had lost only two men. 'Did I tell you the truth?' he asked those that remained.

The Scarecrow Squadron bowed before him. 'You have done all that you promised, General,' they said.

Now they galloped like the wind towards the Yellow River, while the cumbersome Han army struggled in pursuit. At the river bank was a village headman from the further shore who waited with a boat.

'Great General Yu,' he cried, 'I beg you to make haste to cross over! I am the only one who has a boat, so when the Han army arrives they will not be able to follow, and in my country we will gladly make you king.'

Hsiang Yu laughed. 'What good to cross a river when Fate pursues a man?' he said. Then he grew sombre, thinking of the past. 'Once, from your land, I took eight-thousand men to be my soldiers. They crossed the river with me to this shore, but today not a single man of them returns. They rot where the grass grows long, or bleach in the desert sun. A general gives what is easy to give: honours and titles. The soldiers give what is hardest to give: their lives. If their fathers and brothers took pity on me now, how could I look them in the face for shame?' Seeing the countryman look sorrowful, Yu dismounted and led forward his horse by the bridle. Dark with sweat, and crusted with the dust of battle, Silver bore himself still like a proud charger. 'For five years,' said Yu sadly, 'I have ridden this horse, and I have never yet seen his equal. Again and again he has borne me scores of miles in a single day. How could I bear to kill him now? His name is Silver and I give him to you.'

Then Yu ordered his men to dismount and drive their horses to safety. Neighing and whinnying at the strange command, the chargers galloped off with empty saddles, to slake their thirst and browse among the thickets on the river bank. 'Now we will advance to meet the enemy face to face with our short swords, hand to hand and foot to foot,' said Yu. The handful of faithful comrades knew this was to be a fight to the death. Before long the advance guard of the enemy came in sight. Yu charged and fought in close combat, until he had suffered a dozen wounds. Then, looking around in the din and dust of the battle, he saw a man he knew well, a Han cavalry officer, Lu. 'We are old friends, are we not?' he called to Lu, who eyed him carefully then said to the Han general, 'That man is Hsiang Yu.'

Yu trod boldly towards them, ankle deep in blood and mud. 'I have heard that Han offers a reward for my head,' he said proudly; 'fifteen-hundred pounds of gold and ten-thousand manors, is it not? I will do you the favour.' With these words, he cut his own throat and died. The Han horsemen trampled over each other to get to Yu's body and tear it apart. The last of his warriors died in the struggle and became captains among the ghosts.

After Hsiang Yu's death, the whole region surrendered and the Lords of Han ruled China. Fathers, mothers, children and wives wept for those they had lost. And Hsiang Yu's army became the dust of the hills and ridges, for none that are born can escape this thing.

THIRD CENTURY B.C.

Where a great battle once was fought,
Strange music sounds from under the ground;
The hooves that hammered, the feet that trod,
Leave their echoes for ever.

11 · The flying horses

In the reign of the Emperor Wu, in the dynasty of Han, barbarian horsemen swept like flood-water over the land. A river of men and horses poured down from the northern hills and spread across China. The sturdy, shaggy horses of the invaders trampled the fields of growing rice; the men set fire to the peasants' huts as they galloped along. The barbarians seized jewels and silk which they crammed into their saddle-bags, they drove herds of stolen cattle before them, they even carried off the beautiful wives and daughters of Chinese noblemen. The flying hoofs of the enemy sounded like thunder over the plains.

That was a time of mourning. But the Emperor Wu, a name which means 'warlike', sent for Chang, his wise counsellor.

'Shall the cities of Han lie bruised under the hoof of the barbarian? Shall the wailing of Tartar flutes be heard in our land?' said Wu. Chang bowed his head before the Dragon Throne, and awaited the Emperor's command.

'Take a hundred followers and cross the great desert,' said Wu. 'Explore the unknown region beyond the bitter lakes, and find allies there, among the people of the West, who will come to the aid of China.'

Chang bowed his head again, in token of submission. He said farewell to his sons and set out from the Western Gate of the city. Months passed, year followed year, but there was no news of him or his company. Then, one day, ten years after his departure, the narrow streets around the palace were alive with whispers.

'Chang is here!'

'Chang the Counsellor has returned!'

'Only one of his followers is with him. The others have all perished in the desert.'

'But Chang is alive! Chang is here!'

In the throne-room, Chang bowed before the Dragon Throne.

'Son of Heaven, I have travelled far to the West, beyond the hills and the desert and the bitter lakes, farther than ever our countrymen have travelled before. I have seen Indians as dark as the night, in robes of flowing white linen. I have seen men whose skin is as pale as milk. . . .'

'Truly these are marvels,' said the Emperor Wu, impatiently. 'But allies . . . have you found allies for China?'

'No man will fight for us, Son of Heaven,' answered Chang. 'Yet I have found allies in the West. Beyond the hills on our borders stretches a great desert, where for hundreds of miles one journeys through parched rocks and naked earth. But all at once one comes to a green valley, full of the sound of running waters; and soon, as one journeys on, one sees the towers and roofs of a city among the trees. This is the city of Ta Yuan.'

'But the allies – the allies?' cried the Emperor.

'In the emerald-green grass of the meadows around this city graze the most wonderful horses in the world,' answered Chang. 'When they gallop one would almost think they fly; their long manes float in the air like wings. Their hearts are noble; for hours they will race across the plain and never pause, until the sweat stands dark upon their chestnut flanks like drops of their own blood. If our Chinese cavalry were mounted on Ta Yuan horses, it would sweep over the barbarians as the wind sweeps over a field of barley. O Son of Heaven, those horses would be better than any other allies in the world!'

The Emperor Wu sent ambassadors to Ta Yuan bearing a priceless gift, a horse made of pure gold. But when the king of Ta Yuan saw it, he leaned back in his throne and laughed.

'What use to me is a horse of gold? Can it gallop and swerve and

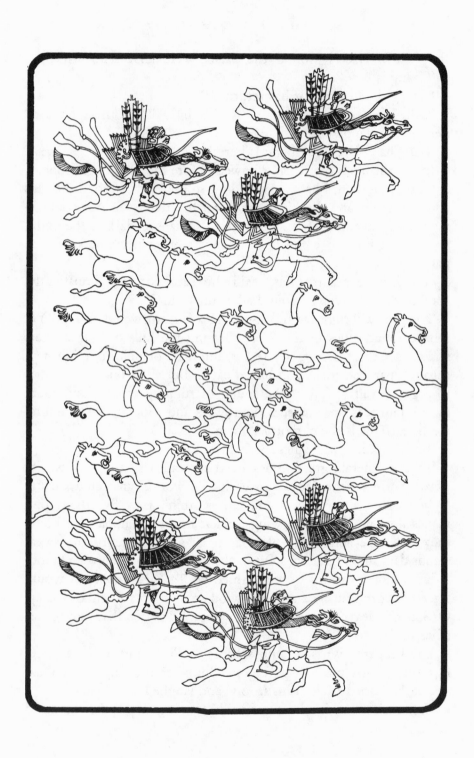

rear and turn, like our own Ta Yuan horses? If I were riding this horse in battle, I should soon be taken prisoner!'

His haughty nobles echoed his laughter. 'We shall not sell our horses! Let the Emperor of China ride his own horse of gold!'

The ambassador was afraid to carry this scornful message to the great Emperor Wu, nor dared he return to China without the horses. That night he crept out of the city with his followers and went to the meadows where the chestnut horses were grazing. Each Chinese horseman carried a spare bridle which he slipped over the head of a Ta Yuan horse. The well-schooled creatures picked their way delicately after the Chinese baggage horses, and the ambassador rejoiced, for he hoped to be out in the trackless desert by dawn.

When dawn broke they found themselves in a rocky valley, at the gate of the desert. The Ta Yuan horses were straining at the bit, longing to gallop, yet held back by the slowness of the baggage animals. They advanced a few more paces, and a distant sound began to beat on the ambassador's ears. First it sounded like hailstones, then like the voice of a waterfall, then like the roaring of a mighty river behind them. It was the cavalry of the King of Ta Yuan in pursuit. In vain the Chinese tore the baggage from their own slow-moving beasts, in vain they climbed on the backs of the Ta Yuan horses; it was too late. Round the bend of the valley, swerving and swift as an arrow of lightning, whirling like a flood, came the horsemen of Ta Yuan.

Only one man returned to China to tell what had happened. The bones of his comrades were picked clean by the buzzards in that far-distant valley.

Terrible was the anger of the Emperor Wu when he heard what had become of his embassy. Soon, by his decree, a great army wound its way out of the land of Han and across the desert. Sunlight glittered on the silver armour of the Chinese knights; the long plumes of their helmets floated scarlet and blue in the desert wind. Peasants stood by the roadside to see them pass, and watched till they vanished into the distance. Yet months passed, and of all that noble army only one man returned.

'Is there a dragon in this western land, which devours my men?'

cried the Emperor, and he sent a fresh army, fifty-thousand strong, across the desert to Ta Yuan. For many months again there was no news, until one evening a weary, foam-flecked messenger rode in at the Western Gate. 'The army of Han has won a great victory, and the people of Ta Yuan have made peace. They have given three thousand horses to the Emperor.'

People crowded out of the city gates shouting, 'The horses are coming! The Ta Yuan horses are coming at last!' Far away on the horizon appeared a speck of dust. It moved; it grew; it swelled to a vast yellow cloud, hanging like a canopy over the swiftly racing army as it drew nearer, nearer to the town. In almost an instant it seemed, so fast did the Ta Yuan horses gallop, they swept in at the city gate. The Chinese horsemen laughed with joy; the plumes of their helmets streamed out behind them like the tail of a comet, and as they galloped they shouted, 'Make way! Make way! Make way for the wonderful horses of the Emperor Wu!'

The Emperor rejoiced when he saw the swift horses which had cost so many lives. 'Now the barbarians will be driven from our land. Honour, glory and long life to the wise Counsellor Chang!' he cried.

But Chang the Counsellor was nowhere to be found, though courtiers and chamberlains scurried through all the rooms of the palace, calling his name. They found him at last in the Imperial stables, watching the horses being rubbed down after their long journey. Their delicate nostrils quivered, they trembled, and the dark sweat stood like blood on their shining flanks. They were even more noble than he remembered them in the emerald-green meadows of Ta Yuan, and as he watched them Counsellor Chang murmured a poem:

FIRST CENTURY B.C.

Gallop, gallop, gallop, horses,
Like a storm of autumn leaves,
Chestnut fetlock, nostril, ear.
Gallop, gallop, horses, gallop,
Safe from danger snatch your man;
Stride a thousand miles of desert;
With the sweat of blood upon you,
Stand at last within your stall.

12 · The secret valley

One morning in spring two young friends set off for a day in the mountains. Their names were Lin and Yuan and they were going to collect the herbs which grow so fresh and green at Bright Weather Time. Some they would chop in the kitchen to flavour broth and salad; others they would hang up to dry in bunches, ready to make medicines as the doctor ordered.

Lin and Yuan spent a happy day. The hours passed swiftly, the Hour of the Rat, of the Monkey, of the Tiger, of the Dragon. When the sun stood highest in the sky they ate their picnic in the shade of an umbrella pine, then they wandered deeper into the hills. The shadows grew longer; the sun began to set. Lin and Yuan turned back towards the town and its sheltering wall. Yet now the trees crowded about them, one exactly like another, and the mountain mist rose cold around their shoulders. Far below, the river roared in its ravine, but they could not see it. Soon they were hopelessly lost. All night they huddled together for warmth, trying to cheer each other with brave words. 'When the Bird of Dawning crows,' said each in turn, 'we shall surely find our way.'

When the sun struck green through the branches, they began to wander. For thirteen days they stumbled over the mountain, tortured by hunger and thirst, chewing pine-kernels, licking the dew from the ferns. The pine-wind mocked their loneliness and despair. Then, on the fourteenth day, they came to a stream, a single thread of clear water running cold over the stones. Lin and

Yuan knelt thankfully down beside it; they were scooping up handfuls of water to drink when they saw something floating downstream towards them.

'Look!' cried Lin. 'What is it?'

'It is a cabbage-leaf,' answered Yuan, 'a freshly picked cabbage-leaf. Cabbages grow in gardens; we must be near some mountain farm.'

'Not a farm but a palace,' cried Lin joyfully, 'for look what is coming now!'

There, bobbing towards them on the stream, was a fluted, translucent cup of precious jade, filled with sesame seeds. The two friends ate the grains and drank from the cup. Then they washed, for they were scratched and dirty from their wanderings, and began to make their way upstream. They entered a gorge, a narrow ribbon of green between high cliffs, which opened at last into a meadow filled with garden plots. It seemed to each that all his favourite fruits and vegetables were growing in that secret valley.

Then two young girls came to meet them, both distractingly pretty in the Chinese style, faces round as the autumn moon, willow-leaf brows, delicate wrists and hands.

'Welcome, Mr Lin,' cried one, and, 'Welcome Mr Yuan,' cried the other. 'Did the stream keep its promise and faithfully bring you the jade cup we sent?'

Lin and Yuan gaped at each other like goldfishes as the charming girls bowed and smiled, quite at ease.

'We have been expecting you for two weeks,' they said. 'Why were you so long in coming to visit our unworthy house?' Their voices played together like a duet of bamboo flutes as they led the way through a house of walls within walls, hidden gardens and shadowy eaves.

'You may call us Bright Cloud and Singing Bird,' said the two ladies. 'These are our waiting-maids.'

With little murmurs of courtesy a crowd of pretty girls surrounded the young men, carrying bowls of rosewater, towels, shell combs and silk pyjamas. Then they led Lin and Yuan like sleep-walkers to the hall where a banquet was laid. Afterwards, the bronze wine-jug went round. 'The spring wind holds a conversation with the strings of my lute,' said Singing Bird. She played an old air, while the waiting maids, gauze sleeves floating around them, danced a courtly dance of long ago. Lin and Yuan felt they must be dreaming long before the maids led them to their curtained alcoves to sleep.

Ten days passed in perfect happiness; then the visitors began to be troubled. 'Our families will mourn for us as though we were dead,' they said. 'We really should go home to them.'

'Don't leave your unworthy friends so soon!' cried the lovely girls, in real distress. Looking down, Lin and Yuan were each amazed to see a bright tear on his sleeve. Of course no young man could resist such charming sorrow, and in the end they promised to stay for six months. Their hostesses used magical powers to make this time delightful.

In the secret valley it was never too hot or too cold, but a soft spring in which the birds sang sweetly. The young men idled all day in silk pyjamas; yet when it was time for a banquet, they found themselves in brocade robes and tall hats, not knowing how they had made the change. One evening there was nothing on the table but a bronze bowl of water. The girls took bamboo fishing-rods and began to angle; soon they were pulling out silver trout, which servants grilled before the visitors' astonished eyes. Another evening, a single jar went round and round the table, yet ended as it had begun, full of clear sparkling wine.

The two girls invented strange games. Once they hid their eyes, inviting Lin and Yuan to fill a box with various small objects then to close it tightly.

'Now we will guess what is in your box,' cried Bright Cloud.

'There are thirteen different things jumbled together,' began Singing Bird. 'The first is a pigeon's egg, the second a piece of red jade, the third a silkworm's chrysalis,' and so on, until she had guessed every single one. The two young men discussed it half the night, but could not think how she saw through the box.

Another time the girls suggested hide and seek. At least we know how to play *that!* thought Lin and Yuan, so they hid their eyes and then set out to look for Bright Cloud. She ran among a flock of sheep on the hillside and turned herself into a white-faced sheep, like all the others. Though she called them with her own voice, teasing and laughing, yet they could not find her anywhere, for she had the power to change her shape at will. And from these games Lin and Yuan guessed that the girls must be fairy princesses.

Next Bright Cloud and Singing Bird promised to teach their friends the Way of Long Life and Happiness. 'Eat and drink health-fully, bathe every day and breathe clear mountain air,' they said. 'Above all, exercise the body, for the hinges of a door, always moving, never grow rusty. We will teach you the Five Animal Antics.' So, every morning, puffing and grunting, Lin and Yuan practised leaping like the tiger, running like the deer, crawling like the bear, climbing like the monkey and flying like the bird. At the end of the six months they looked younger and handsomer than ever.

Yet people tire of pleasure faster than of grief. After the same six months, Lin and Yuan grew homesick. They thought of their mothers' cooking, their little brothers and sisters shouting for piggyback rides, the old dogs asleep in their kennels, and longed for these homely things. They begged to go home, rather afraid the fairies might be angry; but Bright Cloud and Singing Bird were charmingly sympathetic.

'We kept you here to save you from harm,' they said. 'Now the danger is past, you can safely go home. Our servants will see you on your way with music and dancing.'

At the mouth of the Secret Valley Lin and Yuan turned to wave goodbye, but the palace and the princesses had already vanished. Even as they gazed, the music of flutes died away and their fairy escort dissolved into the air.

The young men went thoughtfully on their way. They came to their home town, and stood amazed. There was nothing but a heap of ruins, where rabbits burrowed and quails called in the long grass. Fallen leaves lay heaped against the broken walls, and trees grew through roofless houses. Hidden among them was a hut, where a tiny flame glowed to guide a husband home. A peasant woman answered their knock.

'What brings you to this lonely place, young sirs?' she said.

'The families of Lin and Yuan, where are they?'

'No one of that name here. There are no Lins or Yuans left; all perished in the great earthquake.'

'Earthquake!' cried Lin. 'When was that?'

'Long, long ago,' said the woman.

'Did they *all* die?' asked Yuan, sadly.

'All but two young men who wandered off into the mountains and were never heard of again. But that was two hundred years ago, they must be long since dead.' And with these words she closed the door.

Lin and Yuan went sadly away. The waking world had become like a dream to them and only their dreams seemed real. Each opened his mirror box and looked. Was it his own or another's face that met his startled gaze? Neither could say. Each night they dreamed of the Secret Valley, dream-bodies half way there; each day they watched for a messenger, but of magic wings or bells, still no sound. Year by year, autumn reddened the maples and brought the early frosts; each winter the snow flower fell, hiding the steps and the courtyard.

Slowly they grew old, and one morning they were gone. Was it the common change, or had they gone back to the secret valley of the immortals? What mortal being can tell?

FIRST CENTURY

Perfect happiness – who can ever say it,
Dream it, much less know it?
Taste the fruit – O how sweet, so sweet.
Still, this tang of strange, unforgettable lingering sadness!

13 · The peach-blossom forest

In China, when a man sees a perfect fruit-tree blossoming, he asks the owner of the garden politely, 'Are you perhaps a native of Wu Ling?' He is remembering a story told long ago by the poet Tao Chi'en. If you wish to hear it, this is how it begins.

Yeng was a poor young fisherman who lived in a hut on the edge of the town. One morning, before the sun was up, he woke and, leaving his old parents asleep, went down to the river. On his shoulder sat a sleek black bird with a bronze ring round its neck. This was Yeng's own cormorant, patiently trained by him, which earned enough by fishing to keep all three of them alive in their wretched hut.

The river bank was deserted, for the other fishermen, who had perhaps no old parents to support, were not yet awake. Yeng yawned, and hitching up his ragged trousers with a shudder, for the morning was cold, stepped into his bamboo skiff and pushed off.

The cormorant croaked and shifted from side to side on his thin shoulder. The skiff slid smoothly through the pearl-grey water till they had left the town behind. Far away across the plain, the sun appeared, flooding the river with light and driving the mist from the rice fields. Yeng tilted his bamboo hat to shade his eyes from the sun's rays. It was going to be a hot day.

Presently they began to fish. The cormorant flew low over the water, its sharp yellow eye watching every ripple and shadow. Suddenly it dived and reappeared with a fish in its beak. Yeng called; the bird flew back and – since the tight bronze collar left no room to swallow – dropped its capture in the bamboo basket at its master's feet.

They fished for several hours. On a good day the basket would have been half full of silver and rose-hued fish; but today there were barely a dozen. Yeng thought of his old mother, who dearly liked a slice of pork from the market to eat with her rice, and sighed. He must try further up-stream.

He rowed on, past fields of rice and a bamboo thicket, past a deserted temple and a rocky point, to a stretch of river he had never seen before. The cormorant skimmed away across the water towards a clump of peach trees on the far bank, and came back after only a few minutes with a fine large fish. Yeng rowed as fast as he could towards the spot, but when he reached it, suddenly he felt no desire to fish there. Something drew him as if by magic towards the rosy line of the peach-blossom forest. The peach trees were in full blossom, their boughs trembling with petals. They arched above Yeng's head like a canopy and their reflections curved up to meet them from the still water. He pushed his skiff up the shelving mud and made it fast, then tethered the cormorant and stepped ashore.

A path, scattered with a thousand falling petals, wound its way among the trees. Like a man in a dream Yeng began to follow it. He did not know how long he walked; he only knew that in all his sad, toilsome life he had never seen anything so beautiful. Buds of damask red clung to the rough bark; delicate sprays as pale as sea-shells brushed his cheek; and all around him, like gentle flakes of rosy snow, the petals floated down.

Yeng turned a corner in the winding path and stopped, his heart beating with excitement. The peach-blossom forest, which had seemed to stretch on for ever, ended here. Before him was a rocky cliff, and above him, as high as he could see, towered the steep face of a mountain. But where the path ended was a black crevice in the rock, and it seemed to Yeng as if he heard, from far away through the mountain, laughter and the sound of girls' voices. Gripping the charm he wore round his neck for good luck, he stepped forward into the darkness.

He groped his way along for what seemed a long time. The tunnel began to widen; he could no longer touch the rock walls with his outstretched hands, and in the distance he saw a point of yellow light. He hurried forward over loose stones, while the sound of the girls' laughter grew louder. He broke into a run and, with a suddenness that surprised him, stumbled blinking into a sunlit valley.

'Who are you?' cried two voices together.

'Honoured ladies,' stammered Yeng, bowing low, 'Honoured ladies . . .' and he could say no more.

Before him on the grass, under the shade of a willow tree, two young girls were having a picnic. They had lit a brazier to make tea and each was holding a porcelain cup in her hands. They looked at Yeng with lively curiosity.

'I am Golden Bells,' said the elder of the two, 'and this is my sister, Summer Dress. What is your name?'

'Poor man,' said Summer Dress, 'I believe he is ill. See how thin he is; his face is pale and his clothes are all torn. Do not be afraid, poor man. Tell us your name.'

'Yeng, honoured ladies. Yeng, a poor fisherman,' said Yeng, and looking down at his ragged clothes he blushed for shame.

Perhaps Golden Bells noticed this, for she frowned at Summer Dress and, with a charming gesture of her hand, invited Yeng to sit on the grass beside her while she poured him a cup of fragrant, golden tea. Sipping his tea, Yeng stole sidelong glances at the pair of them. They wore long silk robes embroidered with gold suns. Golden Bells had a coat made of scarlet, and Summer Dress one of leaf-green. Both carried fans, after the manner of the old portraits Yeng had seen when he bore fish to the governor's house in his own town. Their shining black hair was dressed high, in a fashion he had never seen, and fastened with coral pins and combs of jade.

'Where do you come from, honourable Yeng?' asked Summer Dress, who was clearly the bolder of the two.

'From the town, madam,' said Yeng, bowing, cup in hand.

'The town? What town?' The sisters looked at each other, their dark heads tilted like two birds. 'A town?' They frowned. 'We do

not know any town. We live here in the valley of Wu Ling in our
father's house.' They pointed, and Yeng saw brown-tiled roofs
beyond a flowering orange grove.

'Our father is the lord of Wu Ling,' said Golden Bells with dignity.
'Since you are a stranger, we will take you to him.'

'Is he perhaps a magistrate?' asked Yeng with some apprehension,
for he had distasteful memories of these black-gowned gentlemen.

'Magistrate? Magistrate?' Again they looked at each other and
laughed – a sound like clear water running over stones. 'What
strange words this person utters!'

They led the way through the orange trees to the village, and
Yeng followed as though walking in his sleep. Houses, temples, the
very farms by the wayside had the air of five-hundred years ago;
all the people they passed had a smiling simplicity and contentment
he had never seen before. The two girls stopped before a pair of
gates carved with massive stone dragons in the old style.

'This is our home, Yeng,' said Summer Dress.

'Be pleased to enter,' said Golden Bells.

In the cool, shady pavilion they left him to rest. Quiet and smiling
servants set before him dishes of chicken and rice and delicious
young bamboo shoots, food such as Yeng had never eaten in his
life, better even than the dishes he had smelled on his errands to
the mayor's kitchen-courtyard. When he had eaten, Golden Bells
and Summer Dress reappeared. They led him across the courtyard,
past a fountain and a mulberry tree, to a dark pavilion, richly carved.

'Our father commands you to enter,' they said.

Yeng, not daring to look up, stood with bowed head in the
doorway. Silently, as if of their own accord, the double doors shut
behind him and he found himself alone with an old man.

'Approach, stranger,' said an old voice, as dry as rustling bamboo
leaves. 'You are a visitor from the world of toil and sadness; your
face and bearing betray it.'

Yeng continued to look humbly at his own bare feet.

'I pity you,' the old stranger went on, 'but I cannot help you.
You must go back by the way that you came, and never speak of
what you have seen today.'

Yeng looked up to plead; the old man's face was as smooth and quiet as a piece of ivory.

'Five-hundred years ago,' he said, 'my honourable ancestors' – here he bowed to the ancestral tablets set against the wall – 'my honourable ancestors came here to Wu Ling. In the times of trouble, when fathers and brothers were taken to build the Great Wall, they fled to this valley. For five-hundred years we have lived here, maintaining the honourable customs of our forefathers.' He bowed again. 'My people know nothing of sorrow, nothing of strife. We dwell in a fortunate valley and here we shall remain.'

He rose to his feet and Yeng prostrated himself. 'Return, return to your world,' said the old man, 'and swear to say nothing of what you have seen.' Yeng swore – for he was afraid – but knew in his heart that he would not keep his oath.

Next day a magnificent barge sailed up the river. On board were the mayor, the governor, and the magistrate of Yeng's town. Never had the poor fisherman been so important in his native place. They sailed past the bamboo thicket, past the ruined temple and the rocky point. . . .

'Where is the peach-blossom forest?' cried the mayor.

'Where?' cried the governor.

'Imposter!' shouted the magistrate.

They turned on Yeng, but he did not answer them. He was staring stupidly at the mud flats and the empty river bank. The peach-blossom forest had vanished.

FOURTH CENTURY

I was walking in a dream, but the dream was real.
Beauties shook down blossoms from their silk dresses.
Where is it gone? Grey, grey all the long day.
Still on my tear-worn sleeve is one pink petal.

14 · The Land of the Blue Faces

The royal waiting maids stood in a row, the candles shone with a red flame on the palace walls, the musicians played *The Song of the Rainbow Skirts* over again, but the little Princess continued to weep.

'Alas, this person does not wish to marry and go to the Land of the Blue Faces,' she cried. Her lips were painted red and her arched brows blue-black, her glossy plait of hair hung down to her knees and she had a butterfly embroidered on the toe of each shoe; nevertheless she continued to weep.

'Does this weeping become a Daughter of the Dragon Throne?' said her mother, the Empress. 'If it were seemly for wives to choose their husbands, should I have chosen your Imperial Father?'

The waiting-maids turned aside and tittered discreetly behind their wide sleeves, for at this moment the doors were opened and the Son of Heaven came in, followed by his chief minister, carrying a red lacquer casket. 'Most fortunate of daughters,' said the Emperor, settling himself in a chair and smoothing the folds of black silk over his stomach, 'your betrothed, the Lord of Tibet, sends you charming gifts.' From the casket he chose a hair ornament, a tiny silver spear with a carved bird of jade at the tip, but the Princess shook her head and would not even look at it.

'Naturally our child is overjoyed at the prospect of this most honourable marriage,' began the Empress smoothly, but the little Princess flung herself on the ground before her father, sobbing and clinging to his feet. 'Do not send this most unhappy person to the Land of the Blue Faces,' she implored him. 'Is your child never to light the lanterns with you again on New Year's Day, or watch the petals unfurl on the plum-trees in spring? Is she never to hear the orioles sing in the bamboo thicket, or fly kites with the lords and ladies of your court? The people of Tibet have faces tattooed blue, like thieves and murderers in China. They live in huts and wear the skins of animals – indeed it is true, for this person has read it in the *Travels of the Counsellor Chang*. They do not have beds or chairs, but lie on the naked earth. It is even written that they drink milk. Milk! Oh, this one could never endure it!' And the little Princess sobbed more piteously than ever.

Nevertheless, when the day came she was dressed in a coat of red satin with a heavy bridal head-dress of red. Under it she wore the white cotton coat with five corners which a bride must always wear when she goes to her new home. For the last time she knelt to ask her father for his blessing. Then she stepped into her chair with the closed silk curtains and was carried away.

The bearers covered the ground swiftly with their long swinging stride. Sometimes they went through fields, sometimes through forests of bamboo, sometimes beside wide rivers and sometimes across the tawny sands of the desert. But the little Princess was too unhappy even to draw the curtains and look out. She sat, hour after hour, swaying to and fro with the movement of the chair, brooding over the memories of her childhood, which already seemed so far away. After many weeks of travelling they began to cross the great mountain passes. They climbed high, above the stunted pine-trees and the wild rock-roses, until the narrow road ran between cliffs of ice. The little Princess shuddered under her wadded quilts, and when they camped at night she could hardly sleep for the howling of the wind. Presently the road began to wind downhill again, until at last one morning the bearers set down the chair and their leader scratched respectfully with one finger at the curtains. 'See, Daughter of the Son of Heaven,' he said, pointing, 'yonder is the Land of the Blue Faces.'

The little Princess looked out and could hardly restrain a gasp of pleasure. Far below them lay a valley, brimming like a lake with apricot trees in flower. Here and there small terraced fields shone like emeralds in the clear air, and in the depths of the valley a river gleamed. The bearers stumbled on down the mountainside until they came to a village of stone huts, where a little group of peasants stood waiting by the roadside to see them pass. They bowed low, and the Princess trembled, for she expected to see hideous blue faces, but as they raised their heads she saw that they were brown, smooth-skinned and smiling just like the Chinese peasants at home. The women held their children high in the air to wave to her, and the Princess nodded graciously to them in return, as her chair passed by.

The road wound on through groves of mountain trees, until the Princess saw in the distance the walls of a city. Above the battlements the tiled roofs of many houses showed blue and red and green, just like the roofs of the Chinese houses at home. There was even a Chinese pagoda of many storeys, with bells hanging from the eaves. The bearers passed under a high stone arch which spanned the road. One might almost have thought oneself in China, and the little Princess opened her eyes wide in astonishment.

She began to feel less homesick now and to wonder what the Lord of Tibet would be like. 'Probably my lord will be old and ugly,' she thought. 'Perhaps he will have no teeth left, and I shall have to prepare bread and milk for him to eat. Ugh! How will this person endure it?'

Just then her eye was caught by kingfisher flashes of colour ahead, as the great gates of the city swung open and a crowd of people came out. They wore long robes of silk in the Chinese fashion, scarlet and blue and green; they were bowing and waving their hands; and among the hum of many voices the Princess heard the Chinese words constantly repeated, 'Honour and long life to the Lady of Tibet'. The little Princess could hardly believe her ears.

A young man on a sturdy, shaggy pony rode forward from the crowd. His face was brown and his dark eyes were very merry. He pulled off his fur cap and bowed with a flourish, low over his horse's neck.

'Welcome, Daughter of the Son of Heaven,' he cried. 'Welcome to Tibet.'

'Is this really the Land of the Blue Faces?' asked the little Princess; 'or am I perhaps among the people of Wu Ling?'

'Ah, you are admiring our fruit trees,' said the horseman, and the Princess was amazed that a barbarian should know the works of the Chinese poet Tao Chi'en, and the legend of the peach-blossom forest. 'No, honoured Madam, this kingdom is indeed Tibet.'

'But where are the people with blue faces?'

'The Lord of Tibet feared they might frighten you, so he has sent them all away.'

'And may one ask without discourtesy why this town is full of Chinese buildings?'

'The Lord of Tibet feared that you might be homesick, so he has built this poor copy of a Chinese city for you.'

'Yet I seem to see lords and ladies wearing Chinese robes and speaking the language of Han.'

'The Lord of Tibet feared that you might be lonely, so he has ordered his people to copy the Chinese in everything.'

'Pray inform the Lord of Tibet,' said the little Princess, 'that the Daughter of the Dragon Throne wishes humbly to thank him.'

The horseman laughed, and the Princess saw the gleam of his strong, white teeth. 'I am the Lord of Tibet,' he said. 'We have waited a long time for your coming, dear little Princess, and now you are here you are even more beautiful than I had imagined you. Would it please you to ride behind me, on my horse, through the gate of the city, so that my people can see you at last?'

The Princess was secretly delighted, for in all her childhood spent in courts and palaces, she had never been allowed to do such a thing. The Lord of Tibet swung her into the saddle and she clung with both hands to his strong, hard shoulders. A bride must leave her father's house with sorrow, and she still remembered to look a little sad for the sake of appearances but, as they rode into the city, she was happy at heart to be the Lady of Tibet, in the land of the Blue Faces.

SEVENTH CENTURY

There are as many marriages as there are men and women.
One leaves home rejoicing and finds sorrow.
Another goes in tears and regrets – look now!
Her new house is full of laughter and a happy family.

15 · The boy who became a painter

Of all the painters at the Emperor's court the most famous was Han Kan. Princes and mandarins would stand by in wondering admiration as the old artist turned back his sleeves from his wrists, selected a brush from the porcelain jar and set to work with swift, light strokes, while a tree or a waterfall or a prancing horse appeared to grow of its own accord upon the silken page.

Han Kan cared only for painting, and above all for painting horses. When he drew them galloping over the plain or straining at the bridle, it was as though he penetrated to the very soul of these wild, proud creatures. The Emperor, who had commissioned him to paint the Imperial war-horses, often came to watch Han Kan at work; one day he even condescended to criticize.

'Han Kan,' he said, 'you have drawn the neck of my charger, Lo Chei, too long and too arched.'

The mandarins who stood by prostrated themselves, but Han Kan looked the Emperor steadily in the face. 'Son of Heaven,' he replied, 'I have a thousand teachers better than you.'

The Emperor's face grew dark with anger for a moment, but curiosity overcame him. 'Who are they, honourable artist?' he asked. 'And where in my kingdom do they dwell?'

'Be pleased to follow me, O Son of Heaven,' said the old man as he led the way without more words to the Imperial stables behind the palace. There, he went from stall to stall, stroking the glossy flanks and strong withers of the Emperor's horses.

THE BOY WHO BECAME A PAINTER 89

'Unworthy pupil that I am, allow me to present my teachers,' he said, as from his wide sleeves he brought out quinces and apricots, and tender bamboo shoots; while the thousand horses, who knew their old friend well, turned their heads and whinnied softly at his approach.

The Emperor was a wise man who knew when to withhold his anger. 'You have answered me well, Han Kan,' he said, 'but how did you learn to learn from the horses?'

'If you will so much honour me,' said the old painter, 'let us walk back together to my pavilion in the Court of Peacock Feathers, and I will tell you as we go.'

It was long ago, long before there was a painter named Han Kan. But in those days there was a small person named Han Kan, a humble pot boy who worked at an inn. This small person's work was to serve the customers with wine and meat, and make a reckoning of how much each one ought to pay. It was a rough noisy life, but this small Han Kan enjoyed it, for he loved to look at all the many people who came to the inn to drink. He liked the peasants who came in after a hard day's work in the fields, broad-shouldered men, with bare brown arms and feet sticking out of their blue shirts and trousers; he liked too the oxen waiting patiently at the door for their master to finish his rice wine and carry the load home. Sometimes a carrying-chair with silken blinds would stop at the door, and out would step a high official of the Emperor's court, his scarlet robes embroidered with stars and butterflies in stiff gold thread. Han Kan would look very hard at these, as he respectfully set a cup of the best wine before the distinguished visitor.

Above all, though, Han Kan loved to watch one of the inn's most regular customers, a tall untidy man, who sat always in the same corner by the brick stove, tossing off cup after cup of wine. This was Wang Wei, the great painter; and since to be a painter was Han Kan's secret dream, he watched this customer with all the reverence due to a departed ancestor's spirit. It must be admitted however that the great Wang Wei seldom paid his bills. The tally on the bamboo screen grew longer and longer, until at last the proprietor was forced to remind him of it.

'Honoured sir, honourable Wang Wei, if your humble servant, the unworthy proprietor of this inn, may insist, your bills. . . .'

Wang Wei, who was in the middle of an interesting discussion with a fellow-artist, grew angry at once. 'Bills!' he shouted. 'What bills?' The other customers put down their chopsticks to listen.

'These bills, honoured sir, for many days and weeks and months of drinking at my inn. You have not paid for any of it,' said the proprietor.

'And why should I?' Wang Wei did not like to be interrupted.

'But honoured sir, my other customers do,' said the proprietor, pleading.

'And why should I behave like your other customers?' shouted Wang Wei. 'I am a painter – I do not need to pay. I will paint you a picture instead.'

'But, unworthy as I am, it is cash that I need, not pictures.'

'You prefer your miserable cash to one of my exquisite pictures! Then you'll get nothing from me – nothing, I say!' The artist was really angry now. With a flourish of his stick that sent a wine cup spinning to the floor he strode out of the room, while the other customers stared after him in astonishment.

'After him, after him, Han Kan!' cried the proprietor, grown very bold now that the stick was no longer describing circles before his nose. 'Follow Wang Wei and do not come back until you have the money. Sit outside his door; never mind what he says!'

'But, sir . . .' Han Kan began in alarm.

'After him! After him at once,' said the proprietor pushing him out into the street.

Han Kan ran as fast as he could; he could just make out Wang Wei far ahead, taller than the crowd, and brandishing his stick as he strode along. He walked so fast that Han Kan came panting up only in time to see him slam and bolt the high iron gate in the wall of his house. There was nothing to do but wait. Han Kan sat down in the dust, with his back against the wall, and prepared to wait a long time.

It was a hot afternoon. The sun shone on the high wall; the tall plum-tree, growing just inside, let a few white petals come drifting down till they settled at Han Kan's feet. Everything was very still.

Suddenly there was a noise, a clatter of hoofs and ringing of bridle bells, that jerked Han Kan to his feet in an instant. A troop of the Emperor's horses swept by, kicking yellow sparks from the stones. Han Kan stared at the wonderful creatures, with their plumy manes, their shining necks and their rolling brown eyes. All too soon for him they cantered round the corner out of sight. The street was quiet again.

But Han Kan could see them in his imagination as if they were still there, and stooping down he began to draw a horse with his finger in the dust. He found it difficult; once he had to rub the dust smooth and start again. He frowned with effort; he did not hear a sound behind him, as Wang Wei's gate swung slowly open.

'Monstrous!' shouted a voice in his ear, and Han Kan spun round in terror, to see Wang Wei himself, looking closely at the drawing. 'Monstrous,' repeated Wang Wei, 'that an artist, who knows so well how to draw the soul of a horse, has been so disgracefully taught in the fundamental rules of draughtsmanship! Whoever taught you should be ashamed!'

'Honoured sir,' said Han Kan, his knees trembling inside his linen trousers, 'please do not be angry with this insignificant small person. No one has taught me.'

'No one, you say?'

'No, sir. I am not an artist, honoured Wang Wei. I am only the boy from the. . . .'

'Never mind who you are,' said Wang Wei, grasping his shoulder. 'Enter my unworthy house.' He pushed Han Kan impatiently through the gate.

'Oh, but honoured sir, I was told. . . .'

'Never mind, honoured drawer of horses in the dust, what you were told,' said Wang Wei, and led him across the courtyard where the plum-tree bloomed, to a pavilion with a green-tiled roof. There on the steps sat a very small girl, grinding a stick of ink on to a wet stone.

'This is my daughter, Plum Blossom,' said Wang Wei. 'She will show you how to prepare the ink for drawing pictures.'

The small girl showed Han Kan with considerable complacency when she saw that he had never seen such a thing before. Then when the whole stick was ground to a smooth black fluid, Plum Blossom set a tall porcelain jar, full of brushes, on the table at her father's side.

'Tell him what they are, Plum Blossom,' said Wang Wei, and she recited: 'This delicate brush, made of rabbit's hair, is for painting bamboos and slender twigs; this, of deer's hair, is for clouds and pavilions; this heavy one, of wolves' hair is for painting mountains.'

'And no artist worthy of esteem should *ever* leave a brush un-washed,' added Wang Wei severely as he put on his spectacles.

The hours passed like an enchantment for Han Kan as he watched the painter at work. Two strokes of the brush, and a mountain appeared, two more, and another peak behind it. The mountains were tipped with snow, a frozen river glittered between them, and far below, at the bottom of the bamboo scroll, one pale green birch-tree showed the coming of spring.

Yet all the time, inwardly, Han Kan trembled. He knew he must ask for the inn-keeper's money, and then Wang Wei would be angry and throw him out into the street again. The question he was dreading came at last.

'What were you doing outside my unworthy gate?' said Wang Wei.

'Oh, sir, I . . . that is . . . I. . . .'

'Yes, go on, boy,' said the painter.

'Oh, sir, pray do not be angry with this person. My master sent me for the money.'

'What money?'

'Oh, honoured sir, if you will only deign to remember, the money for the inn,' said Han Kan; and then broke off in amazement, for Wang Wei suddenly began to laugh, with a noise that set the bamboo brushes rattling in their jar.

'From the inn! My unaesthetic friend the proprietor had you for a servant!' he gasped, using his long silk sleeves to dash away the tears of laughter that were beginning to trickle down his cheeks.

'Forgive me, sir; my master said . . .' began Han Kan, who could see nothing to laugh at.

'Your master? I am your master now,' said the great artist. 'Your *old* master and I are going to have a talk. Yes, and I suppose I had better remember this time to take some cash with me. You are going to cost your practically bankrupt new master a lot of money, Han Kan; but he remembers that you really used your eyes to look at the horses, and he thinks – yes, he *thinks* – that he will make a painter of you in the end.'

The Emperor of China and the old painter entered the Court of Peacock Feathers, moving noiselessly in their satin slippers. 'And that was how I learned to paint: from my honoured master the great Wang Wei, but before him from your beautiful horses, O Son of Heaven,' said Han Kan. Then, with a respectful bow of his white head, he went up the steps of his pavilion, and, dipping a fresh brush in the ink, began work on his picture again.

EIGHTH CENTURY

A blossom rocking through air, a spark flashing from hoof,
The plip-plop of a bird alighting on a twig,
Can these things that go as soon as they come
Really have existed? There they stand in the picture.

16 · The Moon in the Yellow River

No emperor of China was more glorious than Hsuan Tung of the house of T'ang. Though on the borders war never ceased, yet within the Great Wall all were brothers. There was peace over shining stream and lake, over river-valley green with rice or barley. Before each wayside inn fluttered the wine flag, sign of friendship and good cheer. In the Emperor's own city of Chang An were broad avenues, crowded with courtiers, palace ladies in carrying-chairs, soldiers, priests, painters, poets. The Emperor had thirty-six palaces, with nine-fold gates and cloud towers to admire the view; in his library were two-hundred thousand handwritten scrolls. He founded colleges for astronomy, calligraphy and music, and also a royal school, called the Pear Tree Garden, for young actors and dancers. Even the birds of spring, men said, sang more sweetly in his palace gardens.

In the reign of this emperor, a family named Li lived among the mountains of the west. One night a woman of this family dreamed of a shining white star. The same night she gave birth to a son, and named him Po, which means 'white'. Little Li Po could read at six, though many children of ten could hardly recognize the myriad black characters. At ten he knew whole books by heart, and at twelve began to write poems. Parents of clever children the whole world over plan careers for their sons, sometimes without asking what the boy himself wants. Little Li Po's parents were sure that by the power of the ink-brush he would pass the Imperial

Examinations and leap through the Dragon Gate to the title of Doctor or Master, the black robe and purple sash of a high official.

The Civil Service examinations were an ordeal, needing long and severe study; whole encyclopaedias were written for candidates to learn by heart. 'For ten years,' said a young Master of Arts, 'I never left my books.' When the time came, a boy's parents drove him to the examination halls, where he was shut in a solitary cell for several days to write five essays on current affairs, five on the Chinese classics, questions on mathematics, science and law, an elegant composition in prose, and an original poem. Many came out pale and weeping, knowing that they had failed.

The thought of this and of long years in a dusty government office to follow filled young Li Po with horror. So at fifteen he simply left home. 'For several years I was a vagabond and never set foot in any town,' he said. He met a hermit, with whom he went to live in a hut on the Eastern Cliff to the north of his home. Here the two friends kept wild birds which came at their call and fed from their hands without fear. The mountain mists were high, the cliffs steep; far below wound the road by which Li Po had come. Even as he stood at his door, a cloud swept down and at one stroke cut off the world. The governor of the province came to visit the hut and once again urged him to sit for the Examinations for Persons of Exceptional Ability; but Li Po refused. He preferred to sit on a river rock pretending to fish; he never caught anything, but he was perfectly happy. Later he left the mountain, but ever after seemed like some banished immortal, shut out from paradise.

Li Po wandered like a vagabond down the Yellow River. He married, but his wife died young. He began to drink wine, until people called him the Drunken Genius. Years passed in dreamy idleness, except for writing. 'I am thirty,' he wrote. 'I make verses without tiring, while in front of my house horses and carts go by.' He seemed to write as easily as breathing. 'How thin you look,' he teased his friend, the painstaking poet Tu Fu, 'how wretchedly thin! You must have been suffering from poetry again!' He joined a group of friends, called the Six Idlers of the Bamboo Valley, for day-long picnics of music and drinking in the mountains, with thoughts high as the clouds. Sometimes other poets visited, and they strolled arm-in-arm under the trees. Sometimes they visited friends, who brought out amber cups and dishes of green jade; one even built them a Cloud Tower beside the river to drink wine and enjoy the view. On summer evenings they launched a boat on the Yellow River among green sedges and the little waves like dragon scales. They played the flute as the sun sank into the clear water, or pretty slave girls sang to them while the wind blew their song into the night.

In winter, when snow fell or bitter mountain winds blew round the house, the Idlers would mull a bronze jug of wine over the charcoal brazier and pass it around the circle, while reading aloud from old books. In summer, Li Po drank in the garden, while falling petals filled the folds of his gown, waking at sundown to find his jug overturned, his hands full of flowers which he could not remember picking and his guests departed long ago. Or he would drink alone, raising his cup to greet the reeling moon, or bowing courteously to his own shadow. He saw nothing shameful in drunkenness, but an inspired vision. He wrote:

A single cup may rank with life and death;
The myriad things are truly hard to fathom.
Once I am drunk, losing heaven and earth,
Unsteadily I go to my lonely pillow.
Not to know that self exists,
Of all joys this is the highest.

At forty, Li Po visited the Emperor's great capital, Chang An. Tipsy and eccentric, but sociable, he haunted the taverns of the city, with his poems roughly parcelled into a handy scroll. A courtier who read these poems at once sent them to the Emperor, with this letter: 'I have in my house probably the greatest poet who ever lived. I hardly dare speak of him to Your Majesty, because of his one fault. He drinks; to be frank, *he drinks too much*. Yet his poems are exquisite; pray read them for yourself.'

The great Emperor read the scroll and commanded: 'Fetch me the author of these poems at once.'

Li Po's friends and relations were delighted. 'At last,' they said, 'our banished Immortal will have a career worthy of his talents.' They did not know how unchangeable he was.

Li Po began his career as court poet well, with recitals in the Hall of Gold Bells and banquets at the Table of Seven Jewels. He was handsomely treated, as he wrote back to his friends in the country: 'I rode a colt from the Emperor's stable, my saddle studded with white jade. My bed was of ivory, my mat of fine silk – I ate out of a golden dish.' To courtiers, as to everyone, he was unaffectedly friendly. 'Open your heart to me,' he asked a great lord, 'and do not break off our interview because I do not bow deeply enough.' Everyone sighed over the beauty of his poems.

Yet Li Po still loved to escape to some back-street wine shop, where he drowsed and drank the hours away. He stumbled tipsily through the elaborate court ceremonies, and excused himself merely by saying, 'Wine makes its own manners.' Summoned to a royal picnic in the Garden of Tree Peonies, he was too drunk to stand. Court officials threw buckets of water over him until he revived enough to write an exquisite poem in honour of the flowering trees. On another occasion when the Emperor sent for him, Li Po was dragged in between two servants. 'Please, Your Majesty,' he said, 'I have been drinking wine and it has made me drunk, but I will do my best.' Two court ladies held an embroidered screen around him, and a third held the ink-slab, while he composed a poem in praise of courtly life.

Meanwhile, Li Po was not really happy. He hoped for an official position, with a salary, but a respectable civil servant must not get drunk and give away state secrets. He missed the country. Even the spring wind whispering in his gauze bed-curtains seemed a stranger to him. At the thought of the quiet woods, the clear, pebbly stream, the clean breeze in the pine trees, he was near to tears. After three years he gratefully took the purse of money the Emperor offered and retired from court life. He had no job, no career, no official rank. He sighed over the empire's affairs, but was too lazy to improve

them. Occasionally he seemed depressed by his lack of worldly success, but not for long. 'Something troubled me,' he wrote vaguely. 'What was it? I forget. Man passes like a puppet through the dream play we call life.'

Now Li Po lived largely out of doors, wandering on country roads, taking a river journey, sleeping under the stars. His friends were the rivers and hills, clouds and moonlight. He appeared totally idle, yet all the time he wrote. If old friends came to visit him, he would fish in the sleeves of his shabby gown and bring out scrolls of poems. He gave them away to anyone who seemed to care for them, saying hopefully, 'Pray remember your old man; perhaps he'll be famous one day.' All over the thatched hut in the hills his rough drafts lay disorderly in thousands of separate scrolls.

Once a visitor asked, 'Why does a man of your gifts choose to lead this life of poverty?' Li Po answered with a poem.

You ask me
Why do I live
On this green mountain?
I smile, no answer,
My heart serene.
On flowing water
Petals drifting
Far away.
This is another earth,
Another sky;
No likeness to that
Human world below.

One summer night, happily drunk, so they say, he took a boat on the Yellow River and drifted along, lost in cloudy dreams. Suddenly, before him, he saw a golden moon which seemed to float on the water. Anyone sober might have thought it was a reflection; but Li Po reached out to embrace it with love, fell from his boat and was drowned in the Yellow River.

EIGHTH CENTURY

Banished from heaven, the poet sees
Heaven reflected in every place.
No wonder the double life he leads
Looks to the world like drunkenness.

17 · The ballad of Mulan

In winter, when frost-flowers cover the shuttered windows and the fisherman's oar breaks the ice with a tinkling sound, comes the time for telling stories. With melted snow the housewife boils fragrant tea for her husband, while the children sit together on top of the brick stove. Then the old ballad-maker knocks at the gate, shambles across the snow-filled courtyard, and sitting down in the firelight begins his story:

> *Click, click, click-click-click,*
> *Quick and slow, slow and quick,*
> *Mulan sits at her parents' door*
> *Weaving her silk for evermore.*

The old ballad-maker curves his hand, as if round a weaver's shuttle, and throws it to and fro, so that the listening children, their father, their mother, and the servants who have gathered gaping seem to see the silk being woven by a young girl. Suddenly he crinkles his parchment face into a thousand sad lines as he asks:

> *Why, what is this? The silk is lying*
> *Tangled and still. Mulan is crying.*

And tears, actual tears, roll down the ballad-maker's face as his voice changes to the faltering tones of a young girl:

> *'Oh! How our land is ruined by war!*
> *Down from the north on China pour*

The Tartar horsemen, fierce, like a flood,
A raging river, a river of blood,
Drowning our peace. It tears down the peach,
The willow, the silkworm mulberry. Each
Home is a charcoal ruin, hut,
Or hall, or carved pavilion. But
The Emperor says this must not be.
The Emperor sends a high decree
To every town and village round
The whole of China, at the sound
Of which all run and listen. This
Is what it says: "Our Empire is
In danger. Every man must go
To fight the Tartars and to throw
Them out of China. Young men and old,
All, from all families, all are enrolled!"
All men! Oh then I knew that sorrow
Would wake with me as I woke tomorrow.
Last night I looked, I looked at the roll –
My father's name stood black on the scroll!'

Her father! That is who Mulan weeps for.
These are the special tears she keeps for
Him. Her father is sun and moon
And stars to Mulan. Now, soon, soon,
He will march off in soldier's dress,
Never come back, unless, unless. . . .

Now the ballad-maker nods and shrugs mysteriously as he speaks
in Mulan's voice again, but this time almost in a whisper:

'I must be able to do it, I must!
He who has given me love and trust,
Shall he die and his ashes blow over the plains,
Or drag out his weary life in chains,
A Tartar's prisoner? No, I must save
Him, now, in this hour, as a brave

Daughter should do. I must cloak my face
And ride with the soldiers to take his place!'

Lifting a corner of his ragged cloak sideways across his face, the ballad-maker peeps in and out from behind it, as he speaks first in his own voice and then in Mulan's:

Mulan goes to the Eastern Market!
There she buys a fiery horse.
'Oh my horse, my horse, carry me safely in the cruel war!'
Mulan goes to the Western Market!
There she buys a saddle and horse-cloth.
'O saddle and cloth, sit well on my horse,
That he may carry me safely in the cruel war!'
Mulan goes to the Southern Market!
There she buys a bit and reins.
'O reins and fine silver bit, guide my horse
That he may carry me safely in the cruel war!'
Mulan goes to the Northern Market!
There she buys a tall whip.
'O riding-whip, if need be, lick the sides
Of my fine horse that he may carry me safely,
Safely home again out of the cruel war!'

The ballad-maker puts his finger to his lips and whispers, as all lean forward breathless to hear what Mulan will do next:

Early next morning Mulan arose.
A grey mist like the river flows
Over the hemp fields, and the soft green
Of the mulberry leaves cannot be seen
For large grey drops. All is still.
No one chops wood upon the hill,
Or by the well no one draws water.
Mulan! Take your last look as a daughter
Over your father's home. The pigs
And sheep stir in their pen, the legs
Of the sleeping hens hang from their perch.
All quiet, but now is your time to march,

Mulan! Her flowing silken dress
She hangs on the wall. Instead, a coarse
Thick yellow tunic, leggings bound
With leather, and over all, sweeping the ground,
Her heavy soldier's cloak. Now she
Is like a warrior as can be.
Her face, so marred with weeping, looks
Like a man's too. Down she unhooks
Bridle, saddle, cloth and whip,
Then, while the house is still asleep,
Goes to the wood where secretly
The horse is tethered, sets him free,
Then mounts, and rides him away, away,
Before the red sun lights the day
And she is missed. . . .
Where has she gone?
The army travels all day, on,
On, on, to the north. By nightfall
She camps, already a soldier, her rightful
Place taken – in her father's name –
And no one knows. The camp fire's flame
Flickers by a great river. It is
The Yellow River. The boundaries
Of China used to end here; now
Tomorrow they must cross and go
On, to the war. . . .
The next day, on
And on. Before the misty sun
Has risen, they cross the river. Floods
Sweep men in hundreds away. She goads
Her gallant horse with spur and whip.
He swims and struggles safely up
The farther bank, with her still on
His back. Others are wet to the bone;
But she is warm and dry. She shares
Her rations with her horse, the ears

Of barley given to horses and men,
Mulan the soldier! ....
Now, can you count ten?

The ballad-maker slowly stretches forward his bony knuckles from his wide blue sleeves. One by one, as if they were marionettes worked by wires, his ten fingers jerk stiffly upright, each one to represent the passing of a year in the story:

Ten years! It seems a whole life long –
Ten years of war. Only the strong
Are left to fight, those who have trod
Thousands of miles without a road,
Over mountain, torrent, desert, in ice
Freezing like armour, under skies
Now hot like a bronze gong, now cold
As echoing iron, young men grown old,
Fighting and wandering, men – and one
Besides – Mulan! Yes, though the sun
Has scorched her, the rain has beaten, the wind
Hardened her skin. You hardly find
A trace of her girl's face. She is
The captain of mighty victories,
A hundred attacks and battles done,
The leader of brave men.

Without warning, the ballad-maker spins on his heel, snapping his fingers for joy:

It is won,
The war! The war is over! The foe
Is fled at last, and all may go
Free to their homes!

Then the ballad-maker leans forward once more, and puckers his old face into a living question-mark:

Will Mulan remain
A soldier ever, a leader of men?

The Emperor offers riches galore
To Captain Mulan, his warrior,
Lands, wealth, power. Still with gruff voice
Captain Mulan proclaims his choice:
'Nor riches, lands, nor wealth, nor power,
But leave to return to her maiden's bower!
Return – and be a girl once more!
A girl once more at her parents' door!'

The children clap their hands for glee to hear this, but the ballad-maker has not quite finished. He smiles, and asks:

What did her mother and father say
When they heard Mulan was coming? They
Said nothing for tears of joy; they went
To the gate of their house, old and bent,
But in their best silk clothes, with joy.
And here is her baby brother, a boy
Now, a big boy. What does he do?
He takes his knife with a 'Hilloo!
Hilloo!' startling the silly hens;
He makes a dive for the fattening pens
Where the pigs and sheep are kept – a feast,
A gorgeous feast, is the very least
That a boy who is too excited to speak
Should expect for his long-lost sister's sake!

The children laugh as the ballad-maker becomes the boy waving his imaginary knife. Then, like a magician, he changes his whole face and body again, to become Mulan once more, Mulan standing in front of her mirror in her own room:

But can she forget the years that have passed?
A girl again, a girl at last?
By the window she binds her cloudy hair,
Before the mirror, her gold combs there,
She puts on again her silken dress,
And her girl's face, smiling back from the glass

Tells her: 'You are yourself again.
This is your reward – to be Mulan!'

With light, fluttering fingers, the old ballad-maker seems to dress himself in the girl's silken garment. With a girl's step he solemnly breaks into a little dance of joy. Then he seats himself once more and curves his fingers round the invisible shuttle, tossing it to and fro in the firelight:

Click, click, click-click-click,
Quick and slow, slow and quick,
Mulan sits at her parents' door,
Weaving her silk for evermore.

It is the end of the story. The children clap their hands till they are red and stinging. The master of the house gives the ballad-maker a string of cash, and the mistress, throwing another log into the crackling flames, invites him to share their bowl of bean soup before he makes his way across the snow to tell the story of Mulan to another winterbound household.

EIGHTH CENTURY

Who does not remember the old tales?
Fingers of firelight on the wall, lances of sleet on the shutter.
Whoever does not remember the old tales
Has lost the key that opens the door of life.

18 · The Beggar King's daughter

Once upon a time in the city of Hangchow lived a young scholar named Mo Chi. Mo was nineteen years old; he had passed all his examinations and mastered the six polite arts of a gentleman: music, archery, driving horses, mathematics, calligraphy and good manners. Yet his parents were dead and he had no money, so his career did not prosper. Then, like many young men in this situation, he had a good idea.

'Twenty years is the age for a young man to marry,' he said to himself. 'I can't afford food or clothes, but if I marry a rich girl, her family would surely take care of me.' So he went to the go-between, who arranges Chinese marriages, and explained the position. 'I am too poor to buy even the usual presents,' he added, anxiously.

'No need to worry!' said the fat and cheerful go-between. 'I have the very girl for you – a stork among poultry, a moon among stars!' And he hurried off to the house of the Beggar King.

As in all large Chinese cities, the beggars of Hangchow were a powerful class. If anyone refused to give them money, they invaded his house or his office, making rough music with old cooking pots and broken dishes or threatening him with bamboo sticks till he gave them a string of cash to go away. The ruler of this wild band was Chin, whose family for seven generations had been Kings of the Beggars. He kept their filthy rags and bandages, doled out their food and chalk to whiten their faces for begging, and received a share of each beggar's takings. Over the years Chin had grown rich; his barns were full of grain and his purse full of money. He had now no wife and no son, but only one daughter named Green Jade. This girl was now fifteen years old, just the age for a girl to marry. Chin prized his daughter like a jewel and had given her a good education. Green Jade could read the classics, write both prose and verse and sing to the lute. Peacocks and peonies grew from her embroidery needle; she wrote letters of thanks promptly in a clear hand and had excellent manners.

Busily the go-between related all this to Mo Chi, while he described the young man to Chin as 'high-souled as Confucius'. So in the end they arranged the marriage and fixed the day; Chin even bought his cashless son-in-law new silk robes for the wedding. Furnishers draped damask hangings, cooks made a banquet of birds' nest soup, black eggs, chicken with peony roots, ginger, wine and jasmine tea. Chin was delighted that his precious daughter would move in good society at last, so he invited all Mo's fellow-graduates, but none of his own friends and relations, to the wedding.

After the ceremony, when the bride was unveiled, Mo was beside himself with delight. This lovely, graceful girl was his – and she had not cost him a copper cent! Happily, they sat down to the feast. Then, suddenly, from the courtyard outside arose a hideous clatter. Chin turned pale; he knew what this must be. A horde of filthy diseased beggars, clashing bells, gongs, iron pots and rattles, forced their way in. Some did imitations, very good ones too, of cocks crowing, dogs yelping or cats screeching. Others pestered the guests with their practised beggar's whine: 'Father! Mother! Benefactor!'

Through the crowd, a huge man covered in sores advanced on Green Jade and her shrinking bridegroom. 'I'm your Uncle Scabby,' he bellowed. 'Fancy my own niece getting married and not so much as an invitation card for me! Aren't we all beggars together? It's no better to die a rich corpse than a poor one!' He made to embrace the groom, but Mo and his genteel friends had slunk away in terror. The beggars finished up the banquet with appreciative belches and that night Green Jade wept on her sandalwood pillow alone.

Mo Chi returned next morning, outwardly polite but inwardly filled with rage and humiliation. Green Jade did everything she could to please her husband. She bought him books, engaged tutors and kept the house quiet for him to study. She patched his clothes from her own wicker workbasket and unobtrusively made him new robes for feast days. When he was tired she played and sang to him. She urged him to take higher degrees. 'Do not bend your back for five pecks of rice a day,' she said; and Mo recognized that this beggar's daughter was quoting from the classic of Tao Chien.

So Mo passed his doctor's degree. A twenty-two he wore the black gown and purple sash and was appointed to the Emperor's service as Census Officer in a distant province. Yet still, he fancied, people pointed to him in the street and said, 'There goes the Beggar King's son-in-law.' Any sensible man could have seen Green Jade was one of nature's gentlefolk, but Mo despised her for her relations. 'She will be a blot on my honour for the rest of my life,' he thought pompously. What an absurd figure this Mo was!

They set off up the Yellow River for his new post. The boat slid through calm water, by rushes unconcerned. When they came to the Painted Cliff, where Li Po drowned, the moon hung out its one round lamp. Mo Chi could not sleep for worrying about what people would think of him.

'Come and look at the moon!' he urged Green Jade.

They went on deck; it was like a dream.

'Here in the water – this is not the moon,' she thought, remembering the poet. 'The moon is where it always is – in the sky above.'

She, who had never left the city, looked up at the mountains. 'How large the world is,' she thought. 'How small are men and women!'

Beside her, Mo had quite different thoughts. 'Should anyone fall overboard at night,' he said to himself, 'the current would sweep him away and the body would never be found in the whirlpools of the great Yellow River.'

Stealthily he looked around; no one was in sight. Brutally, he caught the young girl by the knees and threw her overboard. For one moment she floated, an airy white nightgown on the flood.

Then she vanished from sight and the boat swept on. Her silly maid-servants cried, then left off; the boatmen looked curious, but Mo gave them silver money to buy wine and they said nothing.

So Mo arrived at his new post, where he lived like a lord, buying silks, furs, gold, jewellery, and giving dinner parties, all on Green Jade's money. He posed as a widower and thought himself very clever.

Yet if you take an ox, you must give a horse, and fate had a surprise for him. In another junk moored by the Painted Cliff, Mo's new superior officer, Lord Hsu, was also travelling to his post. Hsu and his lady had opened their cabin window to the moonlight and were enjoying a quiet cup of wine together when they heard a woman's cry. A boatman, sent to search, came back with the fragile, dripping, trembling body of Green Jade in his arms. A current had swept her on to a sandbank, saving her life but leaving her alone in the world. Bitterly, between sobs, she told the story of her husband's treacherous cruelty, until the older couple felt tears in their own eyes.

Lady Hsu put the half-drowned girl to bed with fur rugs and hot tea. 'Do not cry, my dearest child,' she begged. 'Happily or unhappily, I hardly know, we have no children. Only consent to become our adopted daughter and this story will have a happy ending!'

Green Jade, smiling through her tears, consented. Richly dressed, she travelled with Lord and Lady Hsu to the Governor's Palace, where Mo was now a minor official. There she lived unseen in the private apartments, performing the family ceremonies to honour the ancestral talents, and charming her new parents with her gentleness and good breeding. When they suggested she should take a new husband, she always refused. 'Though of humble birth, I have my own code of honour. I vowed to be faithful to Mo, and I will be true to my promise. I loved him when I was a poor scholar's wife, and I love him still!' With these brave words, the young girl's tears fell like spring rain.

So Lord Hsu looked at his underling and saw Mo, able, ambitious and eager to please. Hsu sighed to himself behind his lordly sleeve and let it be known discreetly that he was seeking a bridegroom for his much-loved only daughter. Just as he expected, a go-between soon appeared with presents and obsequious offers from Mo. Hsu tried to put him off. 'My wife and I could not part with our only daughter,' he told the go-between. 'Her husband must promise to live in our house and be considerate in every way towards our treasure.'

Mo slavishly agreed to every condition. Lord Hsu sighed again; he had grown very fond of Green Jade and knew she deserved a better man. Yet he agreed to name the wedding day and, with his wife, devised a plan to teach Mo a lesson.

The wedding day came. Mo put on his best robes of red brocade; he mounted a white horse with red trappings and hired flute-players to escort him to his new father-in-law's house. His face and figure were as fine as a painting. 'No longer a beggar's son-in-law but a noble lord's,' he said to himself in high glee. As he rode into the courtyard of the Governor's Palace, women greeted him with a wedding song:

> *Golden saddle and prancing steed,*
> *Embroidered cushions in plenty,*
> *From what quarter is this gentleman*
> *Who has come to our gates?*

Mo's followers sang the traditional reply:

> *He is a gentleman of the capital*
> *Who passed his Literary Examination*
> *And so was chosen as Governor*
> *And became a person of distinction.*

Mo was not quite Governor yet but he meant to be one, and anyway this is what the song says. Within the gates waited the bride, in perfumed robes, red jade slippers and red gauze bridal veil. Together they went through the ritual, bowed to heaven and earth, to Lord and Lady Hsu, and to the tablets of the ancestors, whom they courteously told of their wedding. Mo was in seventh heaven of self-importance as he swaggered into the bridal chamber, related to a lord at last. Suddenly, without warning, old aunts and nurses, pretty ladies' maids and pert slave-girls fell on him with bamboo rods. 'Save me! Save me!' cried miserable Mo, but the women only laughed. Mercilessly they beat him until all his fine clothes fell off. At last he lay, grovelling and snivelling, in a miserable heap on the floor.

Then he heard the softest of voices. Surely, he knew that voice? 'Beat him no more,' it said, 'our poor, fine young gentleman.'

Mo looked up, and saw his bride. Slowly she lifted her veil, revealing the features of Green Jade.

'She's a ghost!' shrieked Mo in terror.

'No,' said the stern voice of Lord Hsu, appearing from behind a gold lacquer screen. 'She is no ghost, but our dear adopted daughter, Green Jade, whom we found below the Painted Cliff.'

Then Mo knew he had been found out and his only chance was, as the Chinese say, 'to acknowledge his inadequacy'. He fell on his knees, blubbering. 'I confess my crime, and beg your forgiveness!'

'What does our dear daughter say?' asked Lord Hsu.

Now Green Jade could easily have pretended to forgive her husband at once, but she was too true to hide her feelings. 'My heart is not a mat to be rolled up when you no longer want it!' she cried passionately. 'When you were poor and struggling you made use of me. When you grew successful you thought yourself too good for me. Low born though I am, how could I stoop to love so mean a man?'

Scarlet with shame, Mo clung to her knees and begged for mercy.

'I believe,' said Lord Hsu, 'that my daughter still loves you. But perhaps,' he added ironically, 'our position in society is too humble for you?'

Miserable Mo writhed with embarrassment. 'A beating, a cursing, a bitter shame,' he thought to himself. 'Was it all worth it, just for a change of in-laws?'

In the end Green Jade forgave him, as she had meant to all along. The young couple lived with Lord and Lady Hsu, honoured and respected as their son and daughter. Mo became Lord Mo, a governor himself. Yet he had learned his lesson so well that when

Green Jade's real father, Chin the Beggar King, grew old and sick, Mo took him into his own palace and cared for him to the end of his days.

'Remembering what you have done for me,' he told Green Jade, 'all I can give you is this poor return.' And stooping, he bowed before the Beggar King's daughter.

TWELFTH CENTURY

Never deny; forgive; be patient; hope.
Four fingers on the hand that lacks a thumb
Can still contrive the task of life
Till you would think a new limb grew.

19 · The long-legged barbarians

The old minister, long since retired from all his offices of state, was enjoying the rainy weather at home in his own house. While the grey sleet rattled against the paper windows, he sat up in the bed which his servants had moved over beside the stove, drinking warm wine and listening to the crackle of chestnuts roasting on the hearth. To all these pleasures he had added yet another – that of playing with his grandson, who was five years old.

While the little boy curled up beside him on the coverlet, the old man set to work folding and snipping with his scissors at sheets of black paper such as puppet-makers use. When he unfolded the silhouettes and held them up before the candle-flame, strange shadows began to dance upon the wall, shapes of cockatoos and monkeys, galloping horses and shaggy mountain bears.

The grandson, Master Tortoise, clapped his hands with pleasure. 'Make a man, honourable ancestor!' he cried. The old man snipped away in silence, his scissors flashing in the firelight. When at last he held up the puppet, a grotesque shape, long and spindle-shanked as a heron, began to waver around the room.

'Is that truly a man?' asked the little boy.

'Why, indeed yes.' The old minister nodded his head. 'That is a long-legged barbarian, such as I saw in former times at the court of the Emperor.'

'Tell me, please tell me about them, honourable ancestor,' begged the little boy, and the old man began:

'It was early in the reign of the Emperor Shun. He had commanded cities to be built and mulberry trees to be planted by the banks of the Yellow River, and he had caused to be built for himself a palace of many courtyards and pavilions, richly carved. When the palace was finished he ascended the steps of the Dragon Throne and there sat waiting to receive the homage of all the kingdoms around China.

'Tribesmen came from all corners of the land to bow before him and offer tribute: at the North Gate, Mongol snow-dwellers; at the East Gate, the fishermen and river-pirates of the great waters; at the South and West Gates, tribesmen from the desert and the plains, clad in robes of blue linen. It was these last who brought news of the long-legged barbarians.

' "It is said," they whispered, "that a tribe of men, taller than young trees, is on its way from far in the west to the court of the Emperor Shun. These men appear even taller than they are by reason of the high sheepskin caps they wear on their heads. Their coats are made of skins and their boots of supple red leather. They ride like the wind on their shaggy horses, cracking whips of many thongs as they go, and they are so tall that they can stoop in the saddle at full gallop to seize a glove from the ground between their teeth."

'The Emperor Shun heard this news with consternation, and summoned his ministers at once to the council chamber.

' "If what we are informed is indeed the truth," he said, "there is a grave risk that the Son of Heaven may suffer loss of face. Suppose that these long-legged barbarians, when they see that we are so much shorter than themselves, should refuse to pay homage!"

'The ministers sat in silence like men stunned, until one, quicker of wit than the others, arose and bowed.

' "Will the Son of Heaven be pleased to hear my plan?" he said. "Since these barbarians are so tall, let us build a special audience-chamber to receive them, with pillars so lofty that they seem almost to vanish into the clouds."

'The councillors murmured their approval, but the Emperor still frowned. "This plan will hardly increase our own height," he said.

' "Let the Son of Heaven command that all his court should learn to walk upon stilts," answered the minister readily, "and let the honourable Master of the Dragon Throne himself condescend to take lessons from some wandering acrobat. In this way we shall tower over these barbarians as a lofty pine-tree over a lowly bamboo-shoot."

'Then began a time of woe at the court of the great Emperor. The air was filled with the gasping of portly well-fed ministers as they struggled to walk upon stilts as high as themselves; the carved pavilions echoed with the sound of their groans as they fell, bruising their well-born hind-quarters upon the ground. The Son of Heaven, out of consideration for their feelings, took his lessons alone; but one might hear daily from his apartments the noise of a soft substance encountering a harder, and the loud cries with which the low-bred strolling player, who had been engaged as tutor, strove to encourage his Imperial pupil.

'Nevertheless, in time their efforts were rewarded. When the long-legged barbarians came swaggering into the tall new audience-chamber, they grew strangely silent at the sight of rows of figures in long black gowns, whose heads reached almost to the lofty roof. The Emperor himself towered twice as high as the barbarian chief, who, after a few silent moments, glared around him and spoke:

' "Why is it," asked this impudent fellow, "that if the Emperor of China is so tall, he needs these other lowly pavilions which I see about the courtyard?"

'However, the quick-witted minister, swaying high against a pillar, soon found means to silence him. "Do you not know," he asked, in the manner of one profoundly shocked, "that the Son of Heaven has it in his power to grow tall or short at will?"

'After this, the long-legged barbarians rendered homage to the Emperor, and, having paid tribute of fine leather and cheeses made of mare's milk, rode home across the desert.'

'That was a fine tale!' cried Master Tortoise. 'And what became of the clever minister who outwitted them all? I am sure he has become a great man in the land.'

'He gave up all his offices of state long ago,' answered the old man, 'so that he might be free to devote himself to the duty of telling tales to his little grandson.'

And with a smile, he leaned back upon his pillows, watching the glow of the sun break through the clouds and redden the western window-pane, until he fell asleep.

THIRTEENTH CENTURY

When young, the stratagems of love and ambition;
In middle age, the cares and contrivance of office.
When one is old, these are remembered no more than
A drop of honey recalls the insect that gathered it.

20 · The King
of the Monkeys

On a mountain lay a magic rock which gave birth to a stone egg. Then the egg cracked and out sprang a stone monkey. He learned to walk and run; he leaped and bounded over the hills, drank from streams, picked wild flowers, ate grass and berries. The Jade Emperor on high in the Jade Heaven, ruler of all things, smiled on Monkey from his palace in the sky and said, 'This will be the finest of all earth's creatures.' The other monkeys bowed to him and called him Handsome Monkey King.

At first Monkey was beside himself with delight, but then he grew sad. 'Today I am king and can do whatever I like,' he said, 'but the time will come when I grow old and weak. I must wander to the end of the world, learning how to stay young for ever and escape death.'

So Monkey set off into the world searching for immortality. First he stole a man's clothes and went prancing through towns and cities, imitating the behaviour of human beings. He still had his furry face and snub nose, but still he felt sure he must look civilized and elegant. Next he looked for someone to teach him the trick of immortality, for so he thought of it. 'Would your lessons make me live forever?' he asked a learned teacher.

'To hope for that would be like trying to fish the moon out of the water,' replied the Teacher truthfully. Yet he did teach Monkey to fly through the air on a cloud trapeze, to become invisible, to pass through bronze or stone and to turn himself into seventy-two different shapes. Of course Monkey thought himself very clever then, and showed off in front of all the Teacher's other pupils, until at last he had to be expelled, howling and protesting, from the school.

He went back to the monkey kingdom and organized all his monkeys into an army. Yet he could not find a sword to suit him, so he went to call on the Dragon King of the Eastern Sea, enthroned among all his Crab Generals, Trout Officers and Shrimp Soldiers. There, in the Sea Treasury, was a thick iron pillar about twenty feet long. 'This,' said the Dragon King, 'is the magic rod which dug the River of Stars between the Herd Boy and the Weaving Girl. Also, the Great Yu used it to fix the depth of the rivers and seas. One touch of it is deadly.'

'A useful bit of iron, and just the thing for me!' said Monkey cheerfully, 'but I wish it were a bit smaller.'

At the sound of these words, obediently, the rod shrank.

'Taller!' he ordered, to test it, and the rod grew up to the thirty-third heaven and down to the eighteenth pit of hell. The crabs and shrimps scuttled under the rocks in terror. 'Smaller, smaller, smaller!' shrieked Monkey, beside himself with delight, until the rod shrank to the size of an embroidery needle, which he tucked behind his ear.

Now Monkey had the magic rod, he grew more pleased with himself than ever, and really created havoc. First he bullied the Dragons, pale and trembling, to give him a coat of gold mail, a phoenix-plume hat, and a pair of cloud-stepping sandals. He gave a banquet, at which he got very drunk, went down to the Kingdom of the Dead, and bullied the judges there. Then he tore the names of all the monkeys out of Death's registers, upsetting the balance of nature by making apes immortal. To keep him out of mischief, the Jade Emperor created him Groom of the Heavenly Stables, but Monkey complained this was not a grand enough title for anyone as clever as himself. He overturned the Jade throne and shamelessly declared himself Great Sage, Equal of Heaven.

Armies were sent to subdue him, but with his battery of magic weapons Monkey defeated them all. The Emperor felt he needed

something to occupy his time, so he created him Grand Super-intendent of the Peach Garden, with a palace in the orchard. 'The rank is an exalted one and I hope we shall have no more nonsense,' said the Emperor impressively. Yet he could not help feeling worried.

As for Monkey, he had got exactly what he wanted, for it was well known that whoever ate the heavenly peaches became immortal. So he dismissed the three gardeners, Hoer, Waterer and Sweeper, and, nimble as the monkey he was, climbed the magic trees. He stuffed peaches greedily into his snubby black muzzle. 'Now I can do whatever I like, without any fear of dying!' he said to himself gleefully. So he behaved worse than ever.

The Queen of the Jade Heaven planned a banquet for her birth-day, which fell only once every six-thousand years when the peaches were ripe. Naturally she did not invite ill-mannered Monkey, who was furious when he found out. 'After all, I *am* the Great Sage, Equal of Heaven,' he boasted. 'Why didn't *I* get an invitation?' So he cast a spell which put all the heavenly servants into a deep sleep. Then he scampered to the table, gobbled the food – bears' paws, dragons' livers, roast phoenix and all – seized a jug of Heavenly wine and got gloriously drunk. Next, still tipsy, he blundered into the laboratory where the great sage Lao Tzu manu-factured Immortality Pills. 'I might as well try a pill or two,' said Monkey, and crammed fistfuls into his mouth as though they were peanuts. Then he grabbed the remaining food and drink and somersaulted down to earth to share it with his monkeys. 'No place like home,' he said, as he lolled at the head of his rowdy table.

By now the whole of the Jade Heaven was in an uproar. Dragons, gardeners, servants, rushed to the Jade Emperor to denounce Monkey. The Jade Queen complained of the shambles in her banqueting hall, the Sage complained about his missing Immortality Pills. This time the Jade Emperor was really annoyed. 'Tell the Celestial Detective to arrest that pestiferous Monkey,' he ordered. After a long struggle, Monkey was captured, tried, and condemned to death. The Heavenly Executioners hewed him with axes, stabbed him with spears and slashed him with swords; yet all this had no effect whatever on Monkey.

'It's hardly surprising,' said the sage, Lao Tzu. 'After all, he ate the peaches of immortality, drank the Heavenly Wine and swallowed my long-life pills. He must be impossible to destroy.'

'What are we to do with a fellow like this?' asked the Jade Emperor.

In despair, he sent messengers to see if great Buddha could help. Buddha arrived in heaven and heard a fearful din of Monkey with his magic rod fighting single-handed against the planets, the winds, the thirty-six Thunder Gods and the Celestial Detectives. Buddha ordered the powers of heaven to lay down their arms and called quietly, 'Monkey.'

'What do you want?' shouted Monkey crossly. 'Can't you see I'm in the middle of a battle?'

'Monkey, why are you making such a pest of yourself in Heaven?' asked Buddha calmly.

'I want to be the Green Jade Emperor,' said Monkey without a blush. 'Tell him to clear out and make room for me. If he won't, then I shall go on like this and never give them any peace.'

Buddha burst out laughing – he could not help it.

'After all,' he said, 'you're only a monkey. What magic do you know that would fit you to rule Heaven?'

This was Monkey's cue to show off in his usual style. 'I know all the tricks,' he boasted. 'I can turn myself into seventy-two different shapes and somersault through the clouds ten-thousand leagues at a jump.'

'Then I'll make a bet with you,' said Buddha. 'If you are really so clever – just jump off the palm of my right hand; if you can do it, you shall become Jade Emperor.'

'This Buddha must be a perfect fool,' thought Monkey to himself, 'his hand is only the size of a lotus leaf. You're sure?' he asked.

'Of course I am,' said Buddha.

So Monkey took a deep breath and jumped. He whizzed through the air so fast he looked like a shooting star. He landed on a plain where five pink pillars stuck into the air. 'This is the end of the world,' thought Monkey. 'I'll prove I've been here.' So he wrote on a pillar, "The Great Sage Equal to Heaven reached this place", and, to show he was master, urinated at the pillar's foot. Then he somersaulted back.

'I've gone and come back,' he shouted to Buddha. 'I went to the end of the world and wrote something on a pillar there. Come with me, and I'll show you.'

'No need for that,' said Buddha. 'You've been on the palm of my hand all the time. Just look down.'

And there, on the middle finger of Buddha's hand, Monkey read "The Great Sage Equal to Heaven reached this place".

'Smell,' ordered Buddha. Useless to pretend; there was a pungent smell of monkey urine on the hand.

'There must be some mistake . . .' began Monkey, but got no further. For great Buddha's five fingers closed round him like five tall mountains, penning him in. He had a lot to learn before he got released. Dear Monkey! Like most of us, he thought himself clever, when all he could do was perform a few tricks.

SIXTEENTH CENTURY

Man apes gods;
Monkey apes men.
Some teacher of bad tricks
Must have started this.

21 · The Prime Minister's birthday present

Governor Liang of the Northern Capital had a favourite captain, whose name was Yang Chi. This man's enemies called him The Blue Faced, and indeed his cheeks bore the tattoo marks of a criminal. Nevertheless Liang believed he had been wrongly convicted and had raised him to a position of trust. 'That man understands ten-tenths of everything,' he would say proudly, when he heard his favourite speak of war or political intrigue.

One night, Governor Liang and his high-born lady sat together at rice. 'My lord,' said she, as she poured wine into his cup, 'pray tell us how you attained to the honour of being Governor of the Northern Capital.'

'From my youth upwards I studied the writings of the sages,' answered Liang. 'Also how can I ever repay the favours of the Highest One, your noble father the Prime Minister, which lifted me from the lowly position of a humble government official?'

The lady inclined her eyes towards him, but not with meekness, while her voice was more like the buzz of a stinging wasp than her duty as a wife required.

'Since you do not forget my father's favour, how then have you forgotten that his birthday falls on the fifteenth day of the sixth moon, when summer is at its height? Already the shoots of rice have risen above the spring rains, the young men are treading the water-wheels, and still you have not sent a present to the Eastern Capital for the Highest One, your father-in-law.'

'Alas,' answered Liang, 'I have laid out ten thousand strings of cash upon gold and jewels to offer him, but do not know how to send them safely, since last year my presents were all stolen on the way, and a similar fortune expended in vain.'

The lady pointed down the table. 'You are constantly saying, "That man understands ten-tenths of everything",' she said. 'Let him take the birthday present.' Liang looked where she pointed and saw the blue-scarred Yang Chi.

He sent for Yang Chi and commanded him to take the treasure to the Eastern Capital. Yang Chi bowed.

'I have heard that the treasure which was stolen last year has not yet been recovered,' he said. 'Also the way to the Eastern Capital is by the Yellow Mountain, a place much favoured by robbers. Let my lord Liang appoint some other, more skilful captain to go, and let us talk of pleasanter matters. How agreeably, for instance, the moonlight falls upon the distant temple roofs!'

'Do not talk of other matters,' said Governor Liang sternly. 'It is my will that you should take the Prime Minister's birthday present. I will give you many soldiers to go with you.'

'A thousand soldiers would still be useless, Your Excellency,' replied Yang Chi, 'since when they reach the haunts of the bandits they will all run away.'

'If what you say is true,' said Governor Liang, 'one might as well never attempt to send a present to the Eastern Capital at all.'

'That is so,' agreed Yang Chi politely. 'It is much better never to do so.'

'Nevertheless,' said Governor Liang, 'there must be a way, and I command you to find it. Otherwise I shall be compelled to think that you understand less than ten-tenths of everything after all, and are therefore not fit to be my captain.'

'There is one way,' admitted Yang Chi, 'but it is very difficult. One should take not many soldiers, but few; these few should not be armed but disguised as carriers; the treasure should not be loaded into a decorated chariot, but divided into bundles and carried upon the men's shoulders. Thus secretly one might bear the Prime Minister's birthday present to the Eastern Capital.'

This proposal found favour in the Governor's eyes, and on the next day Yang Chi set out. The gifts were tied in ten separate loads on the backs of soldiers disguised as carriers. With them walked Yang Chi, wearing rope sandals, a robe of blue cotton and a bamboo hat against the sun. In his hand he carried a sword and a rattan whip. It was the middle of the fifth moon and already hard to march in the sun's fierce rays.

At first, as they crossed the plain through farmland and many villages, Yang Chi permitted the bearers to rest in the noonday heat and to travel only in the cool of morning and evening. After some days they passed fewer houses and began to climb step by step up the Yellow Mountain. Now Yang Chi would no longer march except in the middle of the day, for fear of bandits. The sun, as red as copper, stood high in the sky; there was not the lightest breath of wind nor any speck of cloud. The soldiers muttered together, but Yang Chi drove them on. On the fifteenth day they stumbled up a narrow path between high cliffs, where the dust choked them and the stones scorched their feet; but whenever the bearers put down their loads to rest, Yang Chi beat them with his whip and shouted: 'On, on! This is no place to rest! This is the home of the bandits. On, on!'

At the top of the Yellow Mountain was a wood of rustling pine-trees and there, when they reached it, the soldiers dropped their loads and flung themselves down in the shade to rest. In vain Yang Chi cursed them and beat them with his whip; as fast as he beat one to his feet, another one fell down and lay there groaning.

'Travellers have been robbed here in broad daylight! On, on!' he shouted.

'It is too hot.'

'We cannot move.'

'Oh, for a draught of fragrant cooling wine!' answered the soldiers.

As Yang Chi was about to beat them again he caught sight of a shadowy figure among the trees. Drawing his sword he rushed forward and found seven men lying on the ground to rest beside seven loaded wheelbarrows. At the sight of Yang Chi they all leaped up with a yell.

Lightly he took up the Single Tiger Claw position of Kung Fu. He had learned this Peaceful Wisdom of Self-Defence at a monastery where it had been practised for two thousand years.

'Learn the lightness of the bird, the swiftness of the deer, the velvet tread of the tiger,' the old monk, his master, had said. 'Learn also to know others, for that is great wisdom; but to know yourself, that is true enlightenment.'

In many years he had not learned to know himself; yet now he and his Self would soon meet face to face.

'Who are you?' they cried.

'Who are you?' retorted Yang Chi.

'Do not rob us,' implored the men. 'We are seven poor brothers taking dates to sell in the Eastern Capital. We have no money to give you.'

'Ah, then you are only travellers like ourselves,' said Yang Chi. 'For a moment I feared that you were evil men.'

'Evil men!' the date-merchants smiled at this idea, and Yang Chi, reassured, returned to rest with his own men.

After some time they heard a sound of distant singing and a man came over the crest of the hill, carrying two buckets on a shoulder-pole. When he got into the wood, he too set down his buckets and settled himself to rest in the shade.

'What have you got there?' asked Yang Chi's soldiers.

'White wine to sell in the villages,' answered the man with the two buckets.

'Let us buy it and drink!' cried the soldiers, and they were handing over their cash when Yang Chi awoke.

'Stop, stop!' he shouted. 'Do not buy wine on the road, you sheep-witted fellows! How do you know that it is not drugged by robbers to overcome you?'

The wine-seller smiled coldly. 'Since that is your opinion of an honest merchant, I have no wish to sell to you.'

At the sound of Yang Chi's shouts, the date-merchants came out of the wood and wished to buy wine to drink. The wine-seller at first refused, saying, 'Since that traveller says there is a drug in my excellent white wine, I prefer not to sell it.' At length they overcame his protestations, and the seven date-merchants, drinking each in turn, emptied one bucket, while the soldiers of Yang Chi watched them and grew still thirstier and angrier with their captain.

When one of the date-merchants made as if to dip into the second bucket, the soldiers could bear it no longer, and began to complain loudly. 'Oh sir, you have no heart. See, these men drink and are not harmed. If you do not allow us to drink soon, the second bucket also will be emptied, while we shall still be tormented with our thirst. Sir, have pity!'

Yang Chi was himself very thirsty and he thought, 'It is true the date-merchants drank from the first bucket and suffered no harm. Then I have seen one of them dip his cup into the second bucket also. I will allow my soldiers to buy wine, so that I can drink with them.'

Then the soldiers gave cash to the wine-seller, and sat under the trees drinking the cool white wine, while the date-merchants offered them dates to eat, with many exchanges of civilities. Yang Chi also took a cup of wine and a handful of dates, thanking the merchants for their kindness, for the fruit was soothing to his parched throat. When Yang Chi and the soldiers had finished drinking, the seven date-merchants stood watching them. One by one the soldiers and Yang Chi found they could not rise from the ground. Their heads felt heavy, their feet light, and their knees too weak to support them. When they tried to protest, they were too feeble to speak. The date-merchants, when they saw this, pointed it out to each other with many witticisms.

'You may perhaps be wondering,' said their leader courteously to Yang Chi, 'whether we are bandits, and whether the wine you drank was drugged. That is indeed the case; the wine-seller was our accomplice and although the wine was good, since we ourselves drank it to dispel your doubts, the drug was mixed with it when one of our number dipped his cup into the second bucket. Now I fear we must trouble you to give us the Prime Minister's birthday present, which – so we are informed by spies of the utmost reliability – you are carrying to the Eastern Capital.'

With these words the bandits tipped the dates out of their barrows on to the ground and took up the loads of gold and jewels, which had cost Governor Liang so many strings of cash. Then they wheeled the barrows away down the hill, while Yang Chi lay groaning upon the ground.

'Alas,' he said, 'since my face is tattooed with the blue scar, however unjustly, my master Governor Liang will believe that it is I who have stolen the Prime Minister's birthday present. How can I ever face him again, or how can I return to the Northern Capital? It seems that there is nothing for me to do but join this band of robbers myself.'

And as the effect of the drug wore off, Yang Chi arose and set off briskly down the hill after the bandits.

SIXTEENTH CENTURY

*An honest man
In a land of thieves
Is like a peony
In a weed-filled garden.
The same soil cannot
Nourish them both;
But it is seldom
The weeds that wither.*

22 · The kindly ghost

On the banks of the Yellow River there lived a fisherman named Hsu. His grass hut was built in the curve of a bay and his fishing boat moored at his bamboo gate. He earned enough to buy his family food and his joy was to watch his children at their play. 'There are righteous worthies and learned scholars,' he said, 'but to be honest and happy is best. Rice tastes as good from a wooden spoon as from jade chopsticks, and when I cast my one net in the river my heart feels as though I possess a kingdom.' He was that creature, rare as the Phoenix, a happy man.

One night in winter Hsu set out to fish. There was no moon to light his way, but black clouds, rain, the hurried flight of birds, a rising storm. In his straw hat and grass cape Hsu was almost invisible among the tall reeds. Boats tugged at their mooring-ropes, sails hungry to take the wind. The bridge of slippery ropes swayed and groaned at every gust. Far out, Hsu saw a moving point of fire in the dark, the distant lantern of a passing boat. At his feet the river slid darkly away.

Then the storm came. It heaped up the dead leaves in the farmyards and scattered the weed on the ponds. It smelled like a host of tigers and whistled like a thousand pine-trees. 'May no traveller drown on such a night as this!' thought Hsu as he huddled to eat his slice of bread and drink his midnight wine. Moved by compassion, he poured the last of his wine on the ground, saying, 'Drink too, all you drowned spirits of the river!'

The storm blew out; by morning the river ran like grey silk under a sky shadowed with tender cloud. And when Hsu drew in his nets from the still water, he found them full of rainbow river-trout, plump golden carp, even the rare royal salmon. The wicker fish-basket strapped to his back was almost too heavy to carry to market. There, in the pushing, shouting crowd of fishermen, no one had such a catch as Hsu. He went home richer than ever before, with a present of sugar-crystal ginger for the children. Thereafter, every night Hsu poured out some wine on the ground, with the same invocation. And every morning, even when other fishermen caught nothing, his basket was filled to the brim with fresh and gleaming fish.

One night, as Hsu sat watching his lines by moonlight, a young man of old-fashioned elegance appeared, strolling beside the river as though in thought.

'Sir,' said the friendly fisherman, 'since our meeting is an unexpected pleasure, I have no worthy refreshment to offer, but would you care to take a simple cup of wine?'

'You do me too much honour!' cried the young stranger, bowing with old-world courtesy. 'Kindly allow me to drink to your distinguished health.'

'To my shame, I have no scholar's cap and gown,' said Hsu.

'Pray do not apologise,' said the stranger, 'for wisdom may also be read in the book of real life.'

'My point exactly!' cried Hsu in delight. One cup of wine became two, then three, and soon the pair were talking of this and that like old friends. When morning came, both were distinctly tipsy and Hsu had not caught a single fish.

'Forgive this person's foolishness!' cried the stranger. 'I forgot to beat the water for you, as I usually do.'

Before Hsu's astonished eyes, the stranger seemed to dissolve into the air. In a few moments a silver shoal swam down-stream, leaping and cutting the water with shimmering fins. When Hsu pulled in his nets, they were full of fish as usual, all at least a foot long.

Hsu spent part of the money on some excellent wine. Next

evening the moon shone bright, and once again he found the young man sitting idly by the river.

'Nothing my humble self can offer is worthy,' said the fisherman, 'but at least I owe you a fish for supper.' He held out a plump carp in a string bag.

'Indeed you owe me nothing,' said the stranger. 'It is I who have all too often been your unworthy guest, since your first welcome hospitality that night of the great storm.'

In amazement Hsu rubbed his eyes with gnarled fists. 'Until yesterday I had not the honour of knowing you!'

'Then allow me to introduce myself,' said the young man with a charming smile. 'My name is Wang and I am a professional ghost.'

'A ghost!' cried Hsu, jumping back in alarm.

'One of those drowned spirits of the river, with whom you shared your midnight picnics,' explained Wang. 'Long years ago I slipped and fell from the treacherous rope bridge. I am compelled to haunt this river bank until the next traveller drowns and takes my place as resident ghost. My lonely wanderings have often been tedious, but now,' he added with his invariable old-fashioned courtesy, 'I trust we shall pass many delightful nights in fishing and conversation.'

It was impossible to mistrust anyone so genuinely friendly. Night after night the strange pair watched their nets, grilled fresh trout on their camp-fire and shared a jug of mulled wine to keep out the cold. Naturally they talked much of death and hauntings, about which Wang had refreshingly unprejudiced ideas.

'I lived out the years that were given to me,' he said. 'Is not this a reason to be glad?'

Hsu nodded doubtfully.

'Water and ice do not harm one another,' continued Wang calmly; 'life and death are both of them good. The spirit of a person is stored up in his body, like rice in a sack. When the body dies, the spirit scatters, like rice running out of a torn sack. But I apologize for wasting your distinguished time with matters so ordinary.'

Under Wang's influence, Hsu lost all his uneducated prejudices and boldly declared that some of his best friends were ghosts.

Months passed in these agreeable conversations. Then, one evening, the ghost greeted the fisherman with news. 'My friend, we have only this one evening left. I have heard from the Office of Ghosts that my replacement arrives today.'

'Wang, old fellow, I shall miss you,' said Hsu, 'but I mustn't think of my own sorrow. Let's drink a cup to your retirement! Who is to be your successor?'

'Watch a few minutes,' said the ghost, 'and you will see a woman drown. She is the one.'

Before long a peasant woman in ragged blue trousers came along the path to the bridge. On one arm she held a little child, which clung round her neck, looking around with bright bird-like eyes and chattering in small, clear bird-voice. The mother started along the slippery bridge; the child's weight threw her off balance, she stumbled, clutched wildly at empty air and fell into the water. The child's chatter turned to terrified screaming as they sank and rose again. Hsu watched in anguish. He was fond of children and wanted to rescue the poor woman, but if he did, what would become of his friend Wang's substitute? Suddenly Wang vanished. As though by magic, the woman floated to the river bank, where she scrambled ashore, still holding her child, and stumbled dripping back towards the village.

Wang reappeared, looking slightly embarrassed. 'We meet again, old friend,' he said. 'No need to talk of parting, for I don't know when this foolish person will get another chance.'

'But the woman was drowning!' cried Hsu.

'I know.' The ghost blushed, so far as a ghost can blush. 'She had already taken my place; but the Office hadn't warned me she would be carrying a child and I could not bear to hear it crying, so I rescued them both.'

'You are too good!' cried Hsu, and Wang seemed almost to apologize for his kindness.

'After all, two ghosts are not needed to do the work of one. Next time I promise to be more realistic.'

It was some months before his next chance came. 'This time it will be a man carrying a heavy iron cooking-pot on his head,' explained Wang. 'This will cause him to overbalance, fall into the river and drown.'

In a few minutes, the man with the iron pot appeared. 'Why, I know him!' exclaimed Hsu, incautiously, as the man drew nearer to death, step by step. 'He is the only child of aged parents in the next village, on his way to take them food.'

Wang said nothing. Yet when the man slipped halfway across the treacherous bridge, although the heavy pot fell into the river with a resounding splash, its owner recovered his balance like a tight-rope walker in the Imperial Opera at Pekin.

'I should have bitten out this foolish tongue before I told you about his old parents!' cried Hsu, looking accusingly at Wang.

'Filial piety stands first among the virtues,' explained Wang, adding with a wry smile, 'and one's own heart is more dangerous than the Yellow River with all its nine bends.'

Just then the cocks began to crow from the sleeping village, and with tears in their eyes the two friends were forced to say farewell.

Hsu tossed restlessly all day on his straw mattress, worrying about Wang's future. But next evening he found the ghost radiant with good news.

'Head Office has given me promotion!' cried Wang. 'In recognition of my long service as resident ghost here, I have been appointed Official Guardian Angel at the town of Wu Chen. I leave to take up my new duties tomorrow.'

It was a summer night of full moon as the two friends sat together for the last time. A light wind whispered through the tall reeds, ripples rocked the wild duck asleep on the water, and gauzy scarves of mist drifted over the river. Hsu's heart was filled with joy and sorrow, joy for his friend, sorrow for himself. He spoke with difficulty as though a heavy weight lay on his chest.

'The paths of angels and men lit in different directions,' he said with a sigh. 'Shall we ever meet again?'

'What!' cried Wang indignantly. 'You cannot mean to forget our days of friendship? For my part, no official duties will drive you from my thoughts. I promise to watch over you and your household for ever, on my honour as a ghost.'

So, through his guardian angel's protection, Hsu became a rich
and famous fish merchant. When his children were all settled in
life, he used his fortune to build a stone bridge instead of the old
treacherous rope crossing. It spanned the great river like a rainbow
dropped from the sky; on either side the waters shone like glass.
Swallows skimmed under the arches, while above men and women
passed over safely, blessing the names of Hsu the happy fisherman
and Wang the kindly ghost, who met in friendship by the river.

SEVENTEENTH CENTURY

In the spirit all are equal,
Ghost and man, the misty channel
Like a path that both can tread –
No distinction, live or dead.

23 · The faithful wife

In the days of the Ming Emperors lived a government officer named Shen Su. He was a fine young man, not long married to a girl fifteen years old, pretty, so they say, as flowers and jade. She wore a dress of apricot yellow satin and bound up her glossy hair, black as a crow's wing. These two young people lived together as happy as a pair of swallows under the rafters.

Yet favour and ruin change between dawn and dark. The Emperor had a wicked minister named Chou Luan. Men summoned to his office in the morning turned pale and took a last farewell of their families, for they might never return at night. Dukes waited humbly for admittance at the high gates of his palace. No one dared ask how Chou had become richer than any noble in China.

Now Shen Su's work caused him to examine the secret account scrolls at the Board of Ceremonies, and there he discovered how the minister got rich. Chou laid merciless taxes upon the poor workmen and peasant farmers, but kept all the money for himself. In his palace were storerooms crammed with heavy dishes of silver and gold. He also stole ancestral gems and curios from the nobility, threatening them with hired murderers if they refused to hand over their family treasures. All this Su found in the secret scrolls. The young officer was honest as the day and quite fearless.

'A person who has done nothing wrong in the day need have no fear of knocks on his door at night,' he said to himself. So he wrote a report on Chou's malpractices and took it to the Emperor.

Chou roared like a tiger, demanding that Shen Su should be beheaded on the spot for his accusations. This the merciful Emperor would not permit, but he agreed to sign a warrant for the young man's arrest, pending investigations. At dawn next morning, two detectives came to Shen's house. There was hardly time for Shen and his wife to say goodbye.

'Who knows where we shall see the moon next year?' said Shen, face pale and set. 'Do not forget the golden hours that we have shared. If I live, I surely shall return; if I die, remember that all my thoughts have been of you.' Then they took him away, while his young wife watched from her lattice, broken-hearted.

Months passed, the Emperor forgot and Shen still lay in prison. He was locked day and night in a heavy wooden convict's collar, weighing more than thirty pounds and in itself a lingering death. At home his wife ate the bitter bread of sorrow; truly it is said that tears of parting would fill a sea.

Young Madam Shen did not consider herself a clever person, but she knew when a thing had to be done. If she did not send food, her husband would starve to death in his prison-cage. Moreover, for a bribe, the gaolers might unlock his wooden collar at night and allow him to lie down. For food and bribery, she sold her jewels one by one. Next blue willow dishes and jade cups went to the merchant of curios. She cut off her long glossy hair and sold it to make wigs for actors. She sold their house and went to lodge at an inn, filled with noisy drunken travellers. Here she worked day and night with her needle to buy the bowl of rice soup, the lentils, the millet porage, which faithfully every morning she carried to the prison gate.

Years passed. Fifteen times the earth drank the snow, and still by the ill-will of the minister Shen Su remained in prison. To his wife, every day seemed a year. She dreaded the watchdog's bark, for it might mean a messenger to say her husband was dead. She sat alone by her tiny lamp and tried to sew but, weary of work, her hands fell to her lap. 'I know the day he left,' she thought. 'I do not know the year he will return.' Her fingers were numb with cold; the icy scissors slipped from her grasp. 'No one is glad when a girl is born,' she thought. 'She must bow her head and set her teeth to humble herself before strangers. How sad it is to be a woman!'

At night, little sleeping and much grieving, she listened to the cold drip of the water-clock, cutting her heart in two. When night crawled on, her troubled sleep brought dreams of Shen Su. They were saying farewell on a river bank; he was floating down the stream. 'Why does the twilight come so fast? Or is it mist? For I can hardly see your figure in the fast-receding boat!' She woke and wept bitter tears. Yet still her love for Shen Su was like a torch burning clearly through the night.

Meanwhile Shen Su's aged parents still lived. They had no other children and the young wife tried to comfort them. Every spring when the willow buds showed along the canal she said, 'Perhaps this year he will return to us.' At last her father-in-law, who was eighty-seven years old, fell ill. He was as frail as a candle in the wind and she saw with grief that he was near to death. How could he die in peace without a son to close his eyes and follow his coffin to the grave? Her heart turned and turned in her breast like a great wheel. What should she do?

At last she had an idea. This unknown woman wrote a letter to the Emperor of the Dragon Throne, begging to take her husband's place in prison. This is what she said:

'May it please your Majesty. My husband, Shen Su, was imprisoned by order of your minister Chou Luan, and since his arrest fifteen years have passed away. My father-in-law now trembles on the brink of the grave. I am a lone woman, working at my needle to earn our bread. If I nurse his old father, my husband will starve; if I work to feed my husband, his father may die at any hour, alone. Now that my father-in-law is face to face with death, now that my husband can hardly hope to live – I beg you to accept this unimportant person as a prisoner in his place. In this way only can the duties of a son towards his father, and a wife towards her husband, be fulfilled.'

Madam Su wrote the letter, carefully, with many crossings out

Then she made a fair copy and took it herself to the Palace. Bowing to the ground and kneeling humbly before the steps of the Dragon Throne, she laid her scroll at the Emperor's feet.

The Emperor read this letter written from the heart of a simple woman. For every drop of black ink on the rice paper, he saw a scarlet drop of blood, the life blood of a faithful wife. Her plain words moved him as no flowery phrases could have done. For the first time the Emperor began to doubt his minister Chou Luan. He sent secret police to search Chou's house. They returned with baskets full of gold and silver dishes, also stolen jewels, heaped high in his storerooms. Moreover they found secret letters to the enemies of China beyond the Great Wall.

So the Emperor sent for Chou who arrived sleek and smiling as ever. When he saw the heaped-up treasure from his house, and the letters which proved him a traitor, he turned pale, expecting death and torture. Yet the Dragon Countenance greeted him with barbed courtesy.

'Gold is tested by fire and man by gold,' said the Emperor, 'and one seeing is worth a hundred tellings. Let us take pleasure in seeing Minister Chou make a present of his no doubt well-gotten gains to the Imperial Treasury.' Chou, with great effort, achieved a ghastly smile. 'Moreover, in recognition of his long and faithful service, we trust he will accept this unworthy token of esteem.' He waved to a servant to place a silver begging bowl in Chou's reluctant hands. 'This will give the public an opportunity to repay your years of honest toil for their welfare.' He added, behind his fan, 'We have no doubt they will do so with vigour and enjoyment.'

Wretched Chou Luan stumbled into the street with his bowl. There are evil faces which ten coats of mail cannot conceal and his was one of them. At once passers-by recognized their loathed oppressor and began to hurl eggs and tomatoes at him. When he tried to beg, the professional beggars laughed their heads off. Children from the School for Beggars were brought to study him as an example of how not to beg. Everyone in China prudently added a word before his name, calling him Traitorous Chou Luan. No one would put so much as a penny in his begging bowl and he,

who had been the ruin of many good men, died at last of hunger.

In sorrow gold is dull, as Chou learned; yet in joy iron is bright. Shen Su was at once released from his prison cage and set free to return to his father's house. There, under the carved gateway, his wife bowed to greet him, heart joyful, yet full of fears. Would her husband recognize this sad-eyed slave with worn hands and grey hair? Yet, as soon as she saw Su, she forgot her own fears in pity, for this once handsome scholar was a broken husk of a man. Swiftly she ran to support him as he limped over the threshold. In fifteen years the love between them had never been broken by doubt and these two were like the branches of one tree as slowly they went into the waiting house.

SEVENTEENTH CENTURY

When she left her love,
Her hair was black, her lips were red.
When next she met her love,
Her hair was white, her lips were pale.
But fresh as beauty were the tears
That never left her loving eyes.

24 · A case of Magistrate Lan

In the West, when people want to forget their worries, they sometimes read a detective story. In China, for centuries past, they would have read a magistrate story. One of the favourite collections related the inquiries of a provincial magistrate Lan Lu Chow, who was famous for worming out the truth in the most difficult cases. Unlike many judges, Lan would never accept bribes or use torture. Instead he questioned witnesses quietly and kindly, but thoroughly, keeping the court in session till midnight if necessary. All the while he observed not only their speech, but their looks, bearing and character. Then, taking all these into consideration, he judged each case on its merits. This and not any secret magic, as some ignorant onlookers believed, was the basis of the famous Lan method.

One day Magistrate Lan took his seat in the judgment hall, glancing to see that the public scribe was at his table, ink-brush poised, ready to make a full transcript for the Imperial Archives. 'Court be standing on its feet for Mr Magistrate Lan,' shouted the usher. All present clasped hands and bowed respectfully before settling down to listen. 'The first case,' read the usher, unrolling a long parchment scroll, 'concerns a murder at an inn. A drunken brawl broke out in which an onlooker was knocked down. He struck his head against a stone and died instantly. Two brothers who took part in the fight are accused of causing his death.'

'Let the accused be brought into court,' ordered Lan.

Guards led in two young men of about eighteen and twenty,

wearing the high-buttoned tunics of university students. They faced him, silent and serious; yet their bearing was neither furtive nor cowed by their night in the cells.

Magistrate Lan put on his spectacles, a pair of large round tortoiseshell frames containing magnifying lenses, already known in China for a thousand years. Now he could see the defendants clearly. Having studied them, he hooked the eyeglasses half way down his nose and frowned over them severely, knowing from long experience what signs of dismay this caused in the guilty. It was one of his simple tests for clear or clouded consciences. The two students now appeared somewhat blurred round the edges, otherwise, as before, worried, ashamed, yet somehow likeable young men. They winced at the light in a way which reminded the Magistrate of long-forgotten mornings after student parties. Lan called his thoughts to order sharply; in his distinguished career at the bar he had met some charming villains.

'What have you to say for yourselves?' he asked in what the usher called his Number One Stern Voice. Yet his thoughts were elsewhere. He had been educated in the classics; in fact the same usher called him a Walking Library. He loved to turn to his book-case and revisit Li Po or the Great Yu across the years. Now, unbidden, words of Confucius wrote themselves across his mind. 'If I am blunt metal, be my grindstone; if I am in deep waters, be the oar to my boat.'

'What do you say?' he repeated aloud.

'Honoured sir, the case is simple,' answered the elder of the two students promptly. 'By good fortune and good teaching, we unworthy candidates had both just passed our Preliminary Examination, so we went to the wine shop to celebrate. We drank a toast to the great Confucius, then to sage Mencius; the heavens seemed to open around us as we discoursed on this and that. I do not remember what happened, for I was too drunk, but there was a fight. Of one thing I am certain, though. In my carousal I, Elder Brother, hit a luckless fellow-drinker; he fell, struck his head on a cask and was killed, to this intemperate person's deep regret.'

'Sir!' interrupted the younger student hastily. 'The case is as my brother describes, but with one important difference. It was *this* person, Younger Brother, drunk as could be, who knocked the unfortunate man over and killed him. I apologize for my evil deed.'

'Elder Brother is the murderer,' cried the first more loudly.

'No!' shouted the second. 'My brother is innocent. Younger Brother alone is guilty.'

Magistrate Lan sighed; clearly this was going to be a difficult case. 'Let the parents of the accused come before the court,' he said finally.

'Alas, sir,' said the elder, 'our honoured father died when we were children, and our lady mother lives in retirement.'

'Then let her be summoned as a material witness,' said Lan, and stamped the red seal, which alone gave imperial authority to a court order. 'Until she appears, this court will adjourn for the Drinking Tea Interlude.'

In all puzzling cases this admirable Magistrate had well-tried resources for calm of mind. 'Make fresh tea,' he ordered his clerk. 'Be sure that the leaves are supple as a Tartar horseman's boot, unfold like mist rising from a ravine, gleam like a lake and are soft as a garden newly washed by rain.'

The clerk bowed, with a little smile to show he recognized his chief's quotation from the great eighth-century *Tea Classic*. Lan's fondness for tea was well known, and whenever his court was in session the usher kept an iron kettle on the boil over the charcoal brazier in the robing-room.

Soon a servant appeared from the back regions, with Lan's personal bowl of lucent jade, which imparted a delicate tint of green to the tea. Lan held the saucer between thumb and fifth finger, while two middle fingers slid the cover aside, leaving the smallest possible opening so the tea would remain hot. These homely gestures of themselves created a sense of calm and order. Lan sipped delicately, while from the dried jasmine flowers in the tea a faint scent of summer drifted through the room.

Meanwhile the officer of the court rode with his warrant scroll to the pavilion in a bamboo-thicket where the widowed lady lived. He found her painting upon silk, in a studio hung with her own

pictures. Here a solitary traveller on horseback crossed a snowy bridge, there a line of black crows flapped homeward through grey rain. There were pictures of the two defendants as children, playing with pumpkins or red paper umbrellas. Occasionally a picture contained a private joke, as where an author, broom in hand, vaguely attempted to sweep up the muddled calligraphy of his own thoughts. The lady was no common painter for money; her own character was her style. The officer met many people in the course of his duties and was a judge of human nature second only to Magistrate Lan. 'Here is someone attuned to the life-breath of creation,' he said to himself.

The lady made none of the usual fuss with which people receive a summons to court. She put on her padded jacket, ordered the cart harnessed and appeared in court within the hour. She bowed before Magistrate Lan, not with servility, but from respect for his office.

'You sent for me, sir,' she said, and waited gravely.

Lan never hurried or bullied witnesses. He was fond of quoting from the Taoist classics. 'The great secret is to take things with a quiet mind.' Also he had noticed that people given time to think will often tell the truth, whereas in sudden panic they might blurt out a lie. Conversely, a born liar, given time, will betray himself by the extravagance of his inventions. So now, to give the woman time to reflect, he busied himself with taking snuff. This was a lengthy affair. He took out of his sleeve his favourite snuff bottle, made of agate with an engraving of two fishes. He doled out snuff with a tiny ivory spoon, stirred it on a saucer the size of a fingernail, sniffed, and gave a satisfyingly violent sneeze. Even the flies droning on the window-pane were roused by the noise and buzzed angrily over the dusty scrolls. Lan blew his nose on a handkerchief, another useful Chinese invention, and dusted a few grains of snuff from his official robes. All this time, he was covertly observing the witness, her worn, dignified, middle-aged face, her plain dark coat, her strong delicate hands which seemed to have a life and purpose of their own.

'Kindly tell the court your name and calling, madam,' he said.

'I am the widow of Wang Li who was an Imperial Official in this city. Since his death, I have lived in retirement with my two sons.'

'Are you by any chance the Madam Wang whose exquisite paintings have so delighted me?' asked Lan.

The woman answered only with a quotation from the classics which was totally after his own heart. 'There are nine obstacles to becoming an Immortal and one of them is worldly fame.' Yet she could not hide that faint tremor of response which comes from any artist who feels his work has been understood.

'And you are the parent of the accused?'

'While my husband lived,' answered the lady sadly, 'all of us were like the birds of the air: he was the great tree which gave us shelter.'

'And now?'

'I have done my best to bring up his sons as he would have wished; to know what ought to be known and do what ought to be done. Indeed there is no time for anything else.'

'Yet they got drunk and fought in a tavern.'

The mother would not stoop to pleading or excuses. She merely answered, 'We are all human and the highest tower is built on the ground.'

'The Court finds itself in a difficulty,' said Lan, 'since each of these two defendants swears that he alone is guilty and the other innocent. No one on earth knows them as well as you do. Which of them do you believe capable of so grave a misdeed?'

'I do not know,' answered the woman, whose voice at last began to shake a little; 'but I ask you to punish the younger.'

Magistrate Lan was vastly intrigued. 'Mothers usually favour their younger child,' he said, 'and I see frequently before me in court youngest children who are the victims of their parents' deplorable folly in spoiling them. If justice were done, it is the parents who should be punished. Yet you ask me not to spare the younger. Why is this?'

The woman glanced at the younger student, who stood there, strong as a pine tree, clear as water. She closed her eyes and answered firmly:

'I ask you to punish him because he is my own son. The other, his half-brother, is the son of my husband's first wife. When my husband died, he begged me to take care of the boy and I promised that I would. Now, if I let the elder be punished and the younger go free, I should be yielding to my own private love, betraying a promise and wronging the dead.' Now her tears fell beyond concealment and sparkled in the dusty sunshine on the dark stuff of her sleeve.

'Say no more, honoured madam,' cried Lan, waving to the usher to bring her a bamboo chair and a bowl of his own private tea. 'Your truth and loyalty put us all to shame!'

He turned to the two young men, who were hanging their heads in remorse and grief, to see their mother's tears.

'The verdict of the Court is that both are guilty,' he announced, 'and both must make restitution, as the Court determines, to the family of the dead man. Nevertheless, the honourable way you both admitted guilt, your loyalty to each other, above all the example of your mother and step-mother, convinces me that you had no evil intention. The Court therefore pardons you, and reminds you of the Sacred Edict of the Emperor Kang Hsi: "Honour human relationships and above all honour your parents." Do not get drunk at taverns again. Though as a matter of fact, I recollect that when I myself passed my Finals. . . .' Lan hastily took snuff to cover his indiscretion.

'Court dismissed,' said the usher.

EIGHTEENTH CENTURY

A wise man is a walking library.
Experience, his leisurely hand,
Reaches a book from the shelf –
The right one: unhurried, he reads – truth.

25 · Practical Chinese cats

Since I lost my brindled cat,
The rats peer into the stewpot!

So goes the old verse and there are as many tales of clever cats as there are cats' tails in China. Only listen and you will hear.

Once upon a time there lived a happy farmer. Within his bamboo fence and mud wall, he was king. His terraced hills grew beans, corn and maize, tomatoes and green peppers. Even his waste land grew thickets of bamboo-shoots, delicious boiled in the pot in spring. His children drove out the ducks and geese to the pond, and led them home at twilight, safe from the prowling fox. At break of day he shouldered his hoe and trudged out; until yellow evening-cloud he hoed his crops. When he woke at night and heard rain patter down on the thatch, he was happy to think of his thirsty seedlings. It was nothing to him who ruled the land, if his farm was left in peace. He had never wanted to read or write, for, as he said, 'Reading books won't save you from death, and a bowl of rice is what fills the belly.' Yet he knew all the old songs and stories of the countryside by heart. 'I mean to grow old doing as I please,' he said.

Then, suddenly, all this happiness was at an end. For a huge evil rat, larger than a boar, gnawed its way into his barns and devoured all the year's crops which he had stored there. What use to plough and sow, water and weed, simply to make a rat grow fatter? No trap was big enough to catch it, no poison strong enough to kill it, and as for the yellow chow dog, it ran away howling at the sight of that fierce-whiskered snout. The farmer even paid money to a wandering monk who claimed to know a charm against rats. But when the monk beat his gongs, twirled his prayer-wheels and chanted his incantations, the rat merely showed its sharp yellow teeth and gobbled faster than before. The monk went off grumbling. 'Hard to say which of them is the fatter!' thought the farmer gloomily.

Then a neighbour came to the kitchen door, carrying under his arm a small, homely grey cat.

'My unworthy self and humble cat venture to save your honourable home,' said the visitor politely. Even in their trouble, the farmer and his wife could not keep from laughing.

'Why, that poor little creature!' cried the farmer's wife. 'The rat will finish her with one snap of its jaws!'

'I boldly venture to disagree,' said the neighbour.

He set the cat on the table, left the outer door ajar, and nudged them to hide behind the stove. Instantly the rat rushed in snarling and leaped on to the table to devour the cat. The cat jumped to the floor, landing soundlessly on grey velvet paws. The rat jumped after her. Instantly, with no apparent effort, the cat was on the table again, four paws neatly collected, as though on a single cash-piece. The rat charged after her, its mean little red eyes glaring angrily. The cat, with studied indifference, leaped to the floor. This pantomime went on for ten full minutes, while the neighbour, the farmer and his wife watched from their hiding-place. The rat's sides grew dark with sweat, and froth from its ugly jaws spattered table and floor; the three in hiding could hear it gasp at each jump. The cat, by contrast, had not a whisker out of place. The rat dragged itself slowly and heavily to its feet at each fall, until at last it lay panting, unable to move. Instantly the grey cat pounced on it, breaking its neck with one neat nip of her dainty muzzle. Then she jumped back on the table and began composedly washing face and paws.

The farmer and his wife broke into loud cries of thanks and admiration. 'Your wonderful cat has saved our home,' they said.

The neighbour made polite gestures to show that all this was nothing; it would have been exceedingly ill-mannered to praise his own property. Yet he could not deny the cat's cleverness. 'Faithful cat – farmer's friend,' he said.

Emperors as well as farmers need a cat. Hear now how a painted cat brought fame and fortune to a penniless scholar. He had travelled far from home to seek his fortune, without success, for he had only five pieces of cash left, when he came to a large city, where the people spoke a language he could not understand. He wandered through the markets, past inns and temples, blank walls and shuttered houses, until he came to the street of the Sellers of Rare and Precious Curios. Poor as he was, he never could resist these shops. He wandered dreamily into their dusty depths, idly fingering a sandal-wood box, old silk umbrellas, agate snuff-bottles, blue and white ginger jars and a paper fan with a poem written on it, as though the writer's thoughts could be wafted through the air. Suddenly, in a dark and crowded corner, he came face to face with a painted cat. Her picture hung on a long silk scroll, gazing out at him with calm, watchful green eyes. Her white fur looked so soft, he wanted to stroke it. As he looked, the green eyes moved intently; she was watching a mousehole in the corner. At that moment, an unwary mouse looked out. Airy and graceful, the white cat floated out of its picture, neatly bit off the mouse's head, and jumped back into the faded pinks, greens and soft silver-greys of her scroll. A second later, he could almost have sworn she had never moved.

The scholar went to the merchant and held up three fingers. The dealer of course held up ten, but after some minutes of sign language they drank a thimbleful of tea together, to show they had made a bargain. The scholar handed over his last five coppers in the world and went away with the painted cat, neatly rolled round her bamboo batten, under his arm. By narrow paths between towering cliffs he made his way back into the Empire of China. Here the first thing he saw was a notice: 'By order of the Dragon Countenance, fame and riches await the man who can free the Imperial Palace from a horde of *Barbarian Mice*.'

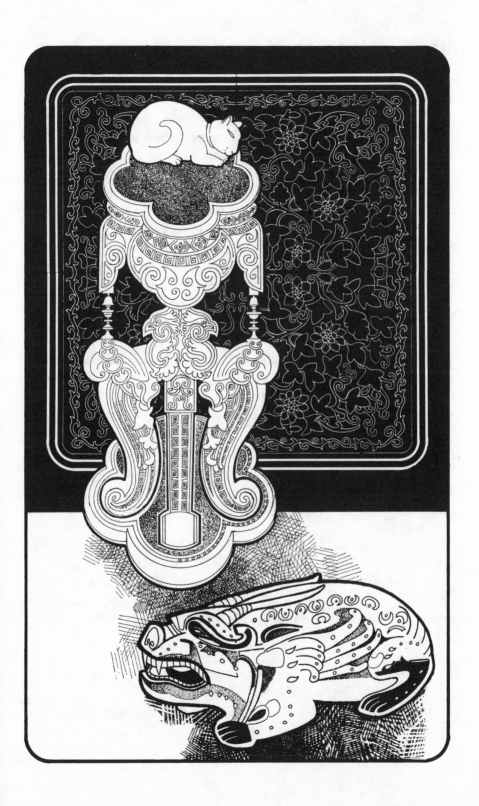

'This scratches me where I itch,' thought the scholar, in the homely phrase he had learned as a child from his old nurse. So, scroll still under arm, he made his way to the capital city.

Then, he went boldly to the palace, presented himself before the Distinguished Lord Chamberlain and requested to be left alone in the Throne Hall at night. This distracted official would have agreed to almost anything, for the mice had frightened the court ladies into fainting fits and made nests in the Imperial Archives. The sun sank, the last red afterglow faded from the western rooms and twilight rustled in the garden trees. Soon, gauze lanterns lit the palace corridors and black night fell. Now the scholar unwound his scroll, taller than himself, and hung it in the deserted Hall of the Dragon Throne. The painted cat looked dreamily out from her silken home.

Suddenly there was a squeaking, a scratching at the wainscot, a scuffling and trampling of tiny feet. The cat's painted ears pricked up, her whiskers quivered, her green eyes shot gold fire. Now, from every hole and corner, an army of greedy mice scuttled over the polished floor. The cat fell on them, silent as summer lightning and as swift, killing them with one nip of her jaws and tossing them away disdainfully. Then, with a gracious wave of the tail, she nosed them into neat rows as an offering for her master. Rank upon rank, the dead mice lay, like a defeated army. As the cat leaped demurely back into her picture, the scholar could have sworn he heard the ghost of a purr.

Now he was richly rewarded and could afford to buy all the scrolls and curios his heart desired. The Emperor created him a Duke and everyone asked him to dinner. Yet his chief delight remained to sit up late by the stove in his study reading old books, while the painted cat hung on the wall and watched her master, as though he too were a mouse.

This friend of man has one enemy; his name is Dog. Here is how the age-old war between Cat and Dog began.

Once upon a time there was a farmer, like our first farmer but richer, who gave his wife a gold ring. But a life of riches is a dream from which we soon awaken – the silly woman lost it! Then what crying and cursing, what shaking of mats, lighting of candles and sweeping of rooms!

Said the faithful yellow chow dog to the fireside cat, 'We must help our god and goddess.'

The cat, who was not a sentimentalist, stretched and yawned. 'What a fuss they make,' she said. 'I know where the ring is, because I can see in the dark. A thief has stolen it and hidden it in a chest.'

'How can we get it back?' panted simple loyal Dog.

'I could get it back if I choose,' said Cat carelessly.

'Oh, you must, you must!' barked Dog.

So Cat caught a mouse but did not kill it. Then she and Dog set out for the thief's house, with the live mouse hanging like a mandarin's moustache from her mouth. They came to a river, and Cat would not get her feet wet. So Dog swam across with Cat on his back; her claws dug into him, but he did not complain. They entered the thief's house. 'Gnaw a hole in that chest,' said Cat.

'I don't want to,' quavered the frightened mouse.

'Then I shall bite off your head,' said Cat sharply, and of course the mouse obeyed. 'Fetch out the gold ring,' she said, and the mouse fetched it, a little dusty, but safe and sound.

Then all three started out for home. The mouse went by underground tunnels and the dog by all the twisting streets and alleyways of the town. But the cat, who carried the ring, went straight over the roof-tops and reached home long before either of them.

Daintily she laid the gold ring at her master's feet. The farmer and his wife were amazed. 'What a clever creature the cat is!' they said. 'We will always feed her and care for her and give her a warm place by the fire.' The cat purred with an air of conscious virtue.

Just then shaggy yellow Dog came panting in at the gate. 'Lazy good-for-nothing beast!' they cried. 'Trust you not to find the ring!'

The dog looked at them with faithful, stupid brown eyes, but could not speak. So they chained him up in the courtyard all night as a guard, and Dog howled to the moon because his god and goddess had forsaken him. But Cat settled down, apparently foot-less, by the fireside, a small furry household deity. She purred and purred and gazed into the flames until her eyes dwindled to two tiny stars, but she said never a word.

In the morning, as soon as Dog was released, he chased Cat. She rushed up a tree and swore at him, her tail bristling like a chimney-sweep's brush. Ever since then, Dog and Cat are enemies.

POPULAR TALES FROM AN
EIGHTEENTH-CENTURY COLLECTION

Since I lost my brindled cat,
The rats peer into the stewpot —
The papers heaped upon my desk
No longer form her pillow,
All the poems I try to write
Now lack her purring music,
When I seek my chilly bed
I miss the fur that warmed it —
Since I lost my brindled cat,
The rats peer into the stewpot!

26 · The Colonel's not for killing

A comedy-thriller with stage directions

A British Consul in China during the 1860s attended this play and greatly enjoyed it. He could not write down the dialogue, but wrote a lively account of all he saw.

The Performance in the open air, begins at six p.m. and ends about midnight.

The Audience apparently one vast family party from great-grandparents to babes-in-arms, and splendid entertainment in itself.

The Dialogue is a skeleton, perfectly filled-out by the actors who have all been thoroughly trained from the age of about nine in mime, ballet, music, voice-production and acrobatics. Each of them knows up to two-hundred plays by heart and there is no prompter.

The Stage is an open platform without curtains or scenery. These would be a waste of time, as the audience can instantly imagine whatever is needed and so marvellous are the actors that it does not feel any lack of setting.

The propertyman or assistant stage manager, in worn black jacket and trousers, moves about the stage placing tables or chairs as needed, catching actors who get killed in the course of the drama, fanning those who look hot in their elaborate costumes, or politely handing a cup of tea to refresh an actor who has just delivered a long speech. When not needed, he sensibly takes the weight off his feet and reads his newspaper, in full view of the audience. Just as the audience can see the invisible scenery, so it does not see this invaluable member of the company!

He enters and sets one chair with two cushions, creating, to our entire satisfaction, the scene of GENERAL YANG'S RECEPTION HALL IN THE CAPITAL.

> [*Enter* GENERAL YANG, *a pompous, cowardly wind-bag of about sixty, in rich robes plastered with Imperial military decorations. He twirls his long, silky moustaches and bows to the audience in an affable yet dignified manner.*]

OLD YANG: Gentlemen – oh, and ladies, of course – I am your humble servant, the famous General Yang, formerly commanding the garrison at the northern pass. Now I am retired and no longer on active service – thank Heaven! In fine weather I fly my kite and when it rains I go out to the wine shop. Meanwhile my son, Colonel Yang, commands my old regiment in the north. I have ordered him to collect tribute money from a fierce tribe of barbarians. I wonder how he likes those howling winds and Tartar swordsmen – ugh! [*He shudders at the thought.*] However, I am sure he is heroically brave [*hastily*] just like his father! He must be fighting in the snow at the Northern Pass this very moment.

> [*Exit. The propertyman stands on a chair and scatters some small pieces of white paper, by which we know instantly that we are in the snowy north. Enter a handsome, not too clever, young army officer, waving a riding whip.* COLONEL YANG *has learned tact and patience from coping with his famous parent. He goes three times round the stage in a zig-zag shuffle to show he is galloping, and dismounts with brilliant conviction from an invisible horse. His manner is courteous and charming, for he is our hero.*]

YOUNG YANG: Charming ladies and distinguished gentlemen, I have the honour to be Colonel Yang, unworthy son of a famous father. I have galloped here to this snowy waste [*he points his riding crop at the scraps of paper*] at my father's command to subdue the northern barbarians, who, so I hear, are commanded by a Tartar princess. They say she wears red leather riding-boots like a man, not little slippers for lily feet like a Chinese lady. I wonder what she is really like?

[*Blast of horn and helpful voice from off-stage.*]

VOICE: Here she comes!

[*Enter* TARTAR PRINCESS, *also on invisible horseback. As she dismounts, we see she is a very tall beautiful girl with long plaits, a feathered hat, riding-breeches and tall boots, which she slaps with her riding crop. She looks around proudly.*]

YOUNG YANG [*to himself*]: I simply *must* be brave; after all, she is only a woman!

[*To Princess*]: I command you to submit and to pay tribute to the Dragon Countenance, Emperor of All China!

PRINCESS [*obligingly, to audience*]: Although a barbarian princess of the utmost fierceness, I am well educated and speak excellent Chinese.

[*To Yang, boldly*]: I defy you and challenge you to single combat!

[*The propertyman hands each of them a wooden sword, and they execute a fight, which is a long drawn pas-de-deux of great style and beauty. At last the princess forces Yang to the ground, a foot on his chest and a sword at his throat. The propertyman fans them both with a large paper fan while the audience applauds enthusiastically.*]

PRINCESS: You are my prisoner!

[*To audience*]: I really ought to kill this young man – but he is strangely handsome. Whatever shall I do? I know!

[*To Yang*]: I will spare your life on one condition – that you marry me immediately.

YOUNG YANG [*to audience, while he gazes raptly at Princess*]: I ought to prefer death to dishonour. I ought, I ought, I know I ought – but what a gorgeous girl she is!

[*To Princess*]: I am delighted to accept Your Majesty's most kind offer.

[*The propertyman hands each of them a cup of tea, and they are sipping happily together, when* YOUNG YANG *suddenly smites his forehead.*]

YOUNG YANG: Oh dear! In all the excitement of getting engaged I forgot! Whatever will Father say when I tell him? [*Exit.*]

[*The capital again: enter* OLD YANG *and* YOUNG YANG, *who wears a dashing little beard to show he has been away for some time. They are obviously in the middle of a blazing family row.*]

OLD YANG: What's this I hear? What do I hear? You actually married this sordid barbarian to save your miserable skin?

YOUNG YANG: You see, Father, I. . . .

OLD YANG: That any Yang, that any son of *mine*, should have sunk so low!

YOUNG YANG: I'm very sorry, Father, but you see. . . .

OLD YANG: I myself would rather have died a thousand times!

YOUNG YANG: I'm sure you would, Father, only. . . .

OLD YANG: No excuses, sir! [*Shouts.*] Guards! Arrest Colonel Yang and take him to the Yamen Gate! Executioner! Prepare for an immediate execution!

[*Two guards seize* YOUNG YANG *and bind him hand and foot with invisible ropes. The executioner brandishes a toy sword, which the ever-helpful propertyman hands him on cue. Just as they prepare to drag their prisoner off, the General's* WIFE *and* OLD MOTHER *come tripping in on their tiny Chinese feet. They kneel before him, wiping ostentatious tears on their long silk sleeves.*]

MADAM YANG: We are the General's long-suffering wife and mother. Spare him! Spare him! Bravest of husbands!
[*To audience*]: Actually, he thinks he's dying every time he sneezes.

OLD MADAM YANG: Spare him! Spare him! Most dutiful of sons!
[*To audience*]: Actually, he used to make a fearful fuss every time it was cabbage soup for dinner.

BOTH: Spare him! Spare him!

[*At this moment two square yellow flags, each painted with a wheel, are carried on stage. Between them, a man in magnificent robes jerks backwards and forwards convincingly.*]

EMPEROR: Honoured patrons of the drama, I am His Majesty the Emperor of All China. Warned by Imperial Carrier-Pigeon that the unhappy Colonel Yang was about to be executed, I have hastened here in the Imperial Chariot to plead for his life. [*In a rather off-hand voice.*] Spare him!

OLD YANG: Your Imperial Majesty's word is law; yet the honour of the Yangs is dearer to me than life itself. The blood of the Yangs is up! The traitor must die!

[*All sob noisily into their sleeves. Suddenly the propertyman clashes two saucepan lids together and all jump in surprise.*]

ALL: Why, whatever was that dreadful noise?

VOICE OFF: It is the noble Tartar Princess, who has come with two captured foreign devils from the West to look for her husband.

YOUNG YANG: Thank heavens – my wife! Perhaps *she* can save me!

[*The entrance of the* PRINCESS *and her two captives is a show-stopper. They are two Western* BUSINESSMEN *in seedy Victorian dress: top-hats, frock coats, pince-nez spectacles, baggy umbrellas, galoshes, etc. Both peer at the Chinese scene with a marvellously accurate parody of Western curiosity and clumsiness. Meanwhile the* PRINCESS *goes through an elaborate series of double-takes with old* GENERAL YANG, *who cringes at the sight of her. He tries to hide behind his sleeve, the furniture, his wife, even the* EMPEROR, *while she stalks him.*]

PRINCESS [*delightedly*]: Why, it's . . . no it can't be! Yes, it is! It really *is*! General Yang himself! [*Heartily.*] Good to see you again, old chap! [*The* GENERAL *groans, but she continues regardless.*] Do you remember how I captured you at the Northern Pass, poor old Yangy? You swore you wanted to marry me, but unhappily you already had a thoroughly unattractive middle-aged wife, not to speak of a tiresome, possessive old mother. [*Both* YANG LADIES *register outrage.*] So I let you off with a simply *enormous* ransom and sent you home with your tail between your legs! [*She cracks her whip at* GENERAL YANG, *who puts his hands over his ears in terror, while the others watch fascinated.*] Why, what in the world have you done with my poor darling little Colonel-Husband? Release him this minute, or I'll skin the lot of you alive, d'you hear?

OLD YANG [*in abject terror*]: Yes, Princess! At once, Princess! Whatever Your Majesty commands!

[*The* PRINCESS *strides to young* COLONEL YANG *and slashes the invisible cords which bind him with her dagger.*]

PRINCESS: My poor, precious little Colonel! Did they hurt you?

YOUNG YANG: Thank you, dear wife, for saving me. I knew you would!

[*He clasps his hands and bows politely, but she puts her arms round his neck and gives him a hearty kiss. The two Western* BUSINESSMEN *giggle and the two* YANG LADIES *faint at this indecent public spectacle. Suddenly the* EMPEROR, *whom everyone has forgotten, stamps his foot with a roar of indignation.*]

EMPEROR: So! General Yang! You would not spare Colonel Yang's life when I, your Emperor, pleaded; yet you granted it at once to this barbarian woman. I hereby create young Colonel Yang General of the West and order him, with his wife, to subdue the Western Foreign Devils. I am sure that she – I mean of course *he* – will win every battle.

[*To audience*]: I wonder if the young lady has any sisters at home who would marry my other generals. I'll speak to the Prime Minister about it tomorrow. [*Loudly.*] As for Ex-General Yang the Traitor, take him to the Yamen Gate for immediate execution.

[*At this the executioner cheers up, but all the other characters fall on their knees and repeat the pantomime of pleading for mercy. In the end the* EMPEROR *mimes that he graciously relents.* OLD YANG *is handed over to his* WIFE *and* MOTHER, *who bully and hen-peck him without mercy while he mops his bald head.*]

OLD YANG: Dear me, it's much easier to command an army than a woman! No doubt that is why there are so many generals in the history books.

EMPEROR: Ex-General Yang, we graciously pardon you in response to the pleas of your family. All the same, we feel seriously annoyed, and to see *someone* executed would soothe our ruffled feelings. [*Thoughtfully.*] Yes, but who shall it be?

[*He looks round meaningfully, while all the characters fall over each other trying to hide, except the two* WESTERNERS, *who have not understood a word. The* EMPEROR *claps hands and points to them.*]

EMPEROR: The very thing!

ALL [*hastily*]: Good idea, Your Majesty! Very good idea! The best idea we've heard for years!

OLD YANG: Or words to that effect!

[*The executioner has been waiting hopefully at the side of the stage all this time. He waves to the guards who bind the* WESTERNERS *with the same invisible ropes they used for* COLONEL YANG, *and sharpens his sword with large stropping gestures.*]

EMPEROR: Off with their heads!

[*The executioner raises his toy sword in a ferocious gesture and brings it very gently down on the necks of the two* WESTERNERS. *The propertyman steadies them as they slide slowly to the ground in highly complicated stage deaths.*]

YOUNG YANG: Long live our Gracious Emperor!

ALL: Long may he reign!

[*The audience is delighted by the execution of the Foreign Devils and the play ends to loud applause.*]

NINETEENTH–CENTURY STAGE COMEDY

The rainbow is illusion.
Sun through water, this we know.
Yet the whole world bathes in colour:
That is the actor's art.

27 · Crossing the Iron Gorge

Early in our own century a long civil war raged in China. Who was to rule this huge, swarming country, the Nationalists and their leader Marshal Chiang, or the Red Army and their General Mao? In the endless fighting, the fields of corn, millet and rice were all blackened by fire, the little huts were burned to the ground and the peasants fled from their homes. It seemed the war would never cease.

At last Mao's army was almost surrounded; in a week Chiang would close in on them. So Mao said, 'We must make a long march, far away from the enemy.' They set off that night, by flaring torchlight. They were not an army, marching in step with flags and drums, but a series of straggling bands. Every man carried a rifle and his own food. They loaded everything they might need, money, cooking pots, guns, on to mule-back. Wives and children rode in carts, knowing they must keep up with the army or be killed.

The first months of the long march, pursued by the enemy, was an endless struggle through rain, mud and darkness. They marched four hours and rested four hours, by day and by night; in rear-guard battles at forts and river-crossings a third of their army was killed. Yet the leaders held a meeting, at which they chose Mao to be their chairman, and ever since the whole world has called him Chairman Mao. Led by him they crossed the Yellow River and at last shook off the enemy at their heels.

Now their enemy was to be mountain crags, river floods, snow and ice. Slowly they began to wind up into the huge mountains between China and Tibet. They halted just long enough to light camp fires, cook whatever food they could find by the wayside and snatch a few hours sleep. Mao slept little. He read the books he carried in the pockets of his shabby blue cotton jacket; he smoked wild tobacco leaves, which he picked beside the trail. Sometimes, sitting with a packing-case as a table by the light of a single candle, he wrote a poem in the old Chinese style:

> *Cold blows the west wind,*
> *Far off in the frosty air*
> *The wild geese call.*
> *Horses' hooves ring out sharply*
> *And the bugle's note is muted.*
>
> *Do not say, 'The pass is defended with iron!'*
> *This very day, at one step,*
> *We shall cross over it.*
> *We shall cross over it!*

The going, through the Great Snow Mountains, the Drum peak, the Pen of Dreams grew harder and harder. It was so high they could scarcely breathe. Hundreds of pack animals lay down in the snow and could not struggle to their feet again. More than half the horses died in whirling hail or snow-storms. The marchers in their thin clothes suffered terribly. Their shoes were worn out, and cold seemed to burn their feet. They wrapped up their legs in rags and straw as a protection against frost-bite. Those who could walk no further had to be left to die. Of all the women who set out on the march, only thirty survived to the end. Yet they were young, hopeful and believed in their cause. The women were even braver than the men; centuries of Chinese history and legends had taught them to endure.

On the frontiers of Tibet they came to a deep river gorge. As they wound in long dragon files along the cliff path by night, their torches sent down arrows of light to glint on black waters far below. They came to a famous bridge, built many hundreds of years before in the old Chinese style. Sixteen heavy iron chains, fastened in the rocks, swung above the dark gorge. Planks laid over them should have formed a path to the other side; but as dawn broke they saw that the planks were gone. The enemy had captured a tower on the far side and stacked the planks there, sure that no one would dare to cross without them.

Now Mao called for volunteers to climb out on the naked chains, seize the planks and re-lay them. Of all the men who offered, he chose the twenty best climbers; not one was more than twenty-five years old. Slowly, hand after hand, foot after foot, they climbed on the swaying skeleton bridge. The chains were cold and slippery to their touch. The wind whistled round them and the black water roared hungrily far below. The young men did not dare to look down, but crawled steadily on.

On the far bank the enemy set up a machine gun and began to fire. Some of the volunteers were hit and plunged to their deaths in the gorge below. Yet still the rest kept on. Now their own side opened return fire, and bullets echoed among the cliffs. At last the enemy fled; the climbers crossed in triumph and seized the fort. An hour later, the planks were back on the iron bridge. By next nightfall the whole army passed over it, singing in triumph.

Slowly they came down from the mountains and rested three weeks in camp. Next, for ten days, they had to cross an endless swamp of black mud, covered by rushes which whistled in the deadly wind. At night it was so cold that they slept sitting roped together in groups for shelter. It was too wet to light camp-fires and they had no rice left, so they ate raw green wheat and the roots of wild turnips. Yet still the survivors kept on.

Now they entered North China, where at last they found food. Rich farmers ran away in terror from the ragged hungry bands, who stole their pigs and sheep and roasted them by camp-fires. On they marched, stronger and happier now. They were struggling along one evening, when a shout went up from the tattered ranks. 'The Great Wall!'

There before them against the northern sky, over hill and valley, ran the huge wall, with its ramparts and towers. They told each other the story of how it had been built, twenty-two-hundred years before, by the First Emperor to keep the barbarians out of China. Mao knew that this sight meant they were near the end of their journey.

Of a hundred thousand who had set out, so it was said, less than twenty thousand arrived. They had travelled nine thousand miles, and had been on the march for a year and five days. Yet as the scattered bands of survivors began to come in, they were confident that, although many years of fighting lay ahead, in the end they would found a new government for China.

Mao was tall and scarecrow-thin with hunger, his black hair untidy, his clothes threadbare. He had lost his few possessions on the journey. Yet, against all the odds, he had led the Red Army through. He looked at the Great Wall in the distance, where so many men had died; yet China still lived. Pulling out the crumpled papers from his pockets, he wrote a poem, to record the moment for ever.

> Lofty the sky
> and pale the clouds.
> We watch the wild geese
> fly south till they vanish.
> We count the thousand
> leagues already travelled.
> If we do not reach the Great Wall,
> we are not true men!

The ragged soldiers cheered hoarsely. There was still far to go, but in their hearts they had reached the end of a great journey.

TWENTIETH CENTURY

> The Great Snow Mountain, the Drum, the Pen of Dreams –
> Words on the map. In blistered feet, hunger,
> Frostbite, terror, the bridgeless bridge,
> Such names are written with the script of death.